2 9 4 8 2 4

HAMMERSMITH
& WEST LONDON
COLLEGE

Gliddon Road, Barons Court
London, W14 9BL
Tel: 0181 741 1688 Fax: 0181 741 2491

For renewals please ask for
ext. 2514

Please renew or return this item by the date below

27 APR 1999		
25 JUN 1999		

CC/593/F&Q/493/MAX

GW00535873

Sam McCarter

For Alison, Deborah and Johnathan

Contents

Section 3: Writing letters

Section 4: Correcting written English

Section 5: Punctuation

Preface

This publication is a self-study book on writing. It is based on the author's work over many years in English as a Second/Foreign Language and English for Special Purposes, first in Sierra Leone, West Africa, and then in the UK.

The book is designed primarily for English language students at an advanced level, i.e. the Cambridge Certificate in Advanced English, Cambridge Proficiency and those students preparing to achieve approximately between 6.0 and 7.5 in the IELTS exam managed and administered by the British Council, the University of Cambridge Local Examinations Syndicate (UCLES) and by IELTS Australia. Native speakers of English may also find some aspects of the book of use.

The book has been written from a cognitive, rather than a grammatical, point of view. The guiding principle throughout is to mimic the underlying mechanisms and thought processes that make up the act of writing. Therefore, it is hoped that if you finish this book you will remember the mechanisms rather than the language and adapt them to suit your own needs.

There are five Sections, focusing on the following areas: coherence in a text, cohesion, letter writing, correcting a text and punctuation. All the exercises may be used in isolation, but you are meant to read them as far as possible in sequence.

The exercises are, in the main, designed to make you slow down and think about organisation in written texts. You may find, therefore, that you have to repeat an exercise several times. On occasion, you may even feel the need to use the Key to help you complete a particular exercise; do not be afraid to do this. The important thing is that you are able to do the exercises with ease after some practice.

One way perhaps to approach the exercises is to think of them as creating a mechanism for you to absorb the information in the Key. Remember that you are also trying to absorb the mental processes involved in writing. This is obviously much more time consuming, and sometimes more frustrating, than learning bare facts. You should not therefore expect to do each exercise perfectly, nor always at the first attempt.

For each exercise in this book you should read all the instructions very carefully.

As you do the exercises try not to mark the book so that you can repeat them.

Sam McCarter
August 1997

Acknowledgements

I would like to thank the following colleagues and friends for their help and support during the writing and production of this book.

Judith Ash, Doris Baybutt, Wendy Bisiker, Julie Easton, Hilary Finch, Caroline Hammond, Phil Jakes, Roger Townsend, Micky Silver and Bernie Wall.

I would also like to thank all those students over the years who have helped in many ways to develop the ideas in this book. It is impossible to name them all, but I would like to name three people in particular: Hiro Khoshnaw, Zoran Momcilovic and Shujaat Al Nathani.

A special thanks is also due to the members, past and present, of the Committee of the Nuffield Self-access Language Project for Overseas Doctors, namely: Anahita Aminossehe, Judith Ash, Alexandra Davies, Stuart Evans, Tony Hooper, Farhad Ibrahim, Dorothy Jones, Joy Parkinson, Juliet Rayner, Wendy Riley, Hernan Rosenkranz, Azar Sheibani, Toni Scott, Robyn Young.

Two members of the said Committee, who are no longer with us, Dr Katherine Elliott and Ken Cripwell, also deserve a mention.

Drs Gill and Bruce Haddock deserve more thanks than I can say for their long patience and forbearance.

Finally, I would like to say a very special thank you to Margo Blythman for having faith.

SECTION 1

a book on **writing**

Contents

a book on **writing**

Exercise 1
How to interpret essay titles

The first step in writing any essay is to read and interpret the essay title correctly. Let us look at the following example:

1. *What steps do you think should be taken to reduce pollution?*

In this essay question, the word <u>steps</u> is the organising word and the general subject is <u>pollution</u>. You do not need to describe pollution itself; the title assumes that you already know what pollution is. The title also indicates that pollution, at the moment, is bad. You could, therefore, use this idea as part of your introduction:

Pollution is nowadays one of the most serious threats to all living things on the planet. There are, however, many steps that can be taken to remedy this situation.

The first sentence is a general statement about the general subject. The second sentence is the topic sentence: it gives the direction of the essay and tells you how to organise it.

Now study the essay titles below and:

(a)   find the word(s) in each question which will help you to organise your essay

(b)   decide what the general subject of the essay is.

---

2.   What are the most effective ways to reduce unemployment in Europe?

3.   What are the disadvantages of using computers in the workplace?

4.   Food additives should be banned. Discuss.

5.   What are the main benefits of investing money in space research?

6.   The main cause of the destruction of the environment is the burning of fossil fuels. Discuss.

7.   Discuss the advantages of sex education in the school curriculum at secondary level.

8.   The best solution to urban traffic problems is to ban all cars from city centres. What is your opinion?

9.   Tobacco advertising in the media should be banned. What is your opinion? Give your reasons.

---

a book on **writing**

Exercise 2
How to link your introduction to your essay title

In the last exercise, you looked at interpreting essay titles and writing a suitable introduction. In other words, you were looking forward from the essay title to the introduction. As you write, however, you also need to look back at what you have written, as well as forward.

In the introductions below, look for the organising words and decide what the general subject is. Then write down a possible essay title for each one.

Example:

> To many people boxing is a cruel sport, which ought to be banned. In my opinion, however, it should not be stopped for many reasons.

If you look at the topic sentence first, you will see that there are several clues to the title. The essay is about your <u>opinion</u> and the <u>reasons</u>. The general sentence shows you that the general subject is <u>boxing</u>. Look at the following titles and you will see that the introduction expresses the general subject and focus or topic of the title:

- *Boxing should be banned. What is your opinion of this statement? Give your reasons.*
- *What is your opinion of boxing? Give your reasons.*

---

1. *Capital punishment is an issue about which people feel very passionately. However, there are many strong arguments against this issue.*

2. *Banning smoking in public places is an issue that gives rise to endless controversy. There are, therefore, many arguments for and against.*

3. *Road deaths in Europe are still a major problem. This situation could, however, be improved enormously by adopting a wide-ranging package of measures.*

4. *Over recent years, poverty has increased in many parts of the world with disastrous consequences.*

5. *The legalisation of cannabis is a subject that has aroused considerable debate. There are, however, a number of benefits to be derived from making the drug legal.*

6. *Recycling waste paper, glass and scrap metal is obviously a sound method for reducing pollution. Even so, a number of equally important measures exist to tackle the problem.*

7. *In some cases a little knowledge is a dangerous thing, but there are also certain circumstances where it can be of enormous help.*

8. *Both public and private means of transport have advantages and disadvantages.*

9. *Corporal punishment, in one form or another, has been part of the educational system in many countries for a long time. As far as I am concerned, however, such punishment is unacceptable.*

10. *Now that oil resources are becoming rapidly depleted, more attention is being focused on alternative forms of energy.*

Exercise 3
Language salvage

Now it is time for you to try to write your own introductions, with some help. All the essay questions below have the same general subject. The focus of each essay, however, is different. In each case, decide first what the focus is. Then look below. You will see that you have a list of introductions with another general subject. Find an introduction, or introductions, with a similar focus and adapt the text to fit the titles.

Example:

1. *Do you agree that euthanasia should be made legal? Give your reasons.*

You can adapt **a** (and also **c** and **h**) as follows:

> *Making euthanasia legal is an issue which arouses enormous controversy. However, I [largely] [dis]agree with such a practice and feel that it should not be legalised.*

---

2. *Euthanasia should be made legal. What are the arguments for and against, and what is your opinion of this statement?*
3. *Discuss the risks of making euthanasia legal.*
4. *How far do you agree with the statement that euthanasia should be made legal?*
5. *Euthanasia should be made legal. Discuss.*
6. *What are the benefits of making euthanasia legal?*
7. *Discuss the advantages and disadvantages of making euthanasia legal.*
8. *What are the arguments against making euthanasia legal?*
9. *What are the arguments for or against making euthanasia legal?*

Introductions:

a. Experimenting on animals is an issue which arouses enormous controversy. However, I largely disagree with such experiments and feel that they should be banned.

b. Experimenting on animals is an issue which arouses enormous controversy. There are, therefore, many arguments for and against.

c. Experimenting on animals for medical purposes is a controversial issue. However, in my opinion, such experiments should definitely be banned for many reasons.

d. Experiments on animals have brought mankind not only many advantages, but also some disadvantages.

e. Although many people are violently opposed to experiments on animals, they have brought many benefits to mankind.

f. Experimenting on animals is a controversial issue. There are, however, many strong arguments against such experiments.

g. Experimenting on animals is an issue which arouses enormous controversy. There are, therefore, many arguments for and against, but, in my opinion, such experiments on animals should definitely be banned.

h. Experimenting on animals is an issue which arouses enormous controversy among the general public. As far as I am concerned, however, such experiments are necessary for a number of reasons and should not be banned.

---

a book on **writing**

Exercise 4
Controlling your ideas

You have looked at how to interpret essay questions. The next stage is controlling your ideas. When you read an essay title, you may sometimes have lots of ideas, but you may not know which of them are relevant.

***

Look at the following titles:

Why do more and more people want to live in cities?

What are the disadvantages of living in cities?

***

Now look at the map below. It shows the general subject, <u>living in cities</u>, and the focus of each essay above: <u>reasons</u> and <u>disadvantages</u>. Around the map is a chaotic jumble of ideas. Look at the jumble and decide which ideas can follow each direction.

List your answer on a piece of paper. **Do not mark the book.**

Exercise 5
How to organise and control your essay

As you develop your essay, you also need to keep your ideas under control. Look at the essay title and plan below:

> *What are the different types of alternative energy?*
>
> As the world looks to a future without oil, more attention is being focused on alternative sources of energy.
>
> The most common form of alternative energy is hydro power.
>
> Another abundant energy source is the sun.
>
> There is also, of course, wind power, of which the best known example is windmills.
>
> As we have seen, there are many different kinds of alternative energy.

If you examine the above plan carefully, you can see:

   (i) the focus word in the title is highlighted. This word shows the specific direction of the essay.

  (ii) the focus word in the introduction is highlighted to show the direction of the essay.

 (iii) each paragraph begins with a topic sentence. In each of these sentences, there is a focus word which links the paragraph to the topic sentence in the introduction and shows the direction of the paragraph. The focus words are also highlighted.

 (iv) the synonyms for the word types: sources, form, energy source, example and kinds. These are interchangeable and help you to avoid repetition of the word type(s).

  (v) the underlined phrases which introduce ideas in the paragraph. Students often complain that they have ideas, but they do not know how to put them down on paper. This inability to introduce ideas is a central problem in writing and, for the most part, goes unrecognised. Compare this with the difficulties you have beginning essays, i.e. writing introductions, and putting your ideas on paper.

 (vi) you have a basic mechanism to help you control your writing.

Now, it is your turn to make essay plans. Below is a short list of essay questions. Work out the focus and the general subject of each essay. Then write an introduction with no more than two sentences and an essay frame for each one as above. Pay careful attention to the way you introduce your ideas in the plan, and also to the synonyms you use. For the synonyms, you may need to use a thesaurus.

1. *Discuss the measures to reduce obesity in rich countries.*

2. *Euthanasia is immoral. Discuss your opinion.*

a book on **writing**

3. *Euthanasia is immoral. Discuss.*

4. *Many people now try to keep fit by jogging or working-out in a gym. What are the dangers of such exercise?*

5. *Some people feel that all medical personnel should be tested for HIV. What would the problems of such a programme be? Give your own opinion.*

6. *Animal organs should not be used for human transplants. What are the main arguments against this statement?*

7. *How can accidents in the home be prevented?*

8. *War can never be justified. How far do you agree with this statement?*

9. *Describe your pet hates.*

Exercise 6
Giving names to sentences

This exercise focuses on the meaning of individual sentences and giving them names. You have, in effect, been doing this already in this Section so far, perhaps without realising.

Sometimes, people have difficulty when they are reading or writing, because they do not recognise the signs in a text which pinpoint meaning. The result is that there is too much unknown information to process at one time. If you learn gradually to recognise text markers, whether they are obvious or hidden, it will improve the amount of detail you are able to process, and absorb. This, in turn, will influence your writing, as you learn to manipulate the signposts you need to mark your own writing.

Look at the sentences below. In some cases, the sentences stand on their own and, in others, they have been removed from a larger text. Give a name to each sentence (e.g. a general statement, a topic sentence, a fact, a suggestion) and give a reason for your answer. Some sentences have more than one name.

Example:

Water boils at 100°C.

The sentence is a fact. Note the use of the Present Simple, <u>boils</u>, which is used to express a fact.

---

1. *The sun rises in the East and sets in the West.*

2. *If only you had come a little bit sooner!*

3. *My main argument for the ban is that personal stereos are a nuisance to all passengers.*

4. *The main argument for the ban is that personal stereos are a nuisance to all passengers.*

5. *Such a policy could, I feel, take quite a few young people off the streets.*

6. *Such a policy would, I feel, take quite a few young people off the streets.*

7. *Such a policy will, I feel, take quite a few young people off the streets.*

8. *These properties could even be renovated by the homeless themselves.*

9. *The most important advantage is the safety of the food.*

10. *As a result, Antarctica will be saved for future generations.*

11. *The law might be difficult to enforce.*

12. *He might have told you about the proposed changes.*

13. *He might have told you about the proposed changes!*

14. *Shaniqua promised to come.*

15. *For example, now it is possible to keep people alive on machines for a considerable time.*

Exercise 7
Naming sentences in a paragraph

This exercise looks at the meaning of sentences as they relate to each other in a continuous text. In other words, you are going to look at coherence in writing a passage.

Read the first two paragraphs of the essay title below. As you read, think about the relationship between the sentences. Then do the exercise which follows.

What measures do you think should be taken to reduce pollution?

(**1**) The very survival of all living things on our planet is now under threat from pollution. (**2**) In my opinion, however, there are a number of very effective measures that can be taken to remedy the situation.

(**3**) The introduction of a carbon tax, i.e. a tax on coal and oil products, such as plastics, petrol and fuel for domestic and industrial consumption, is, I feel, the most important measure. (**4**) Such a tax would have a number of benefits. (**5**) First of all, the reduction in the consumption of fuel would give us fresher air to breathe. (**6**) At the same time, it could raise money for cleaning up the environment and make the general public more conscious of pollution. (**7**) Having said that, however, this tax would be rather unpopular among the general public, as it would reduce their spending power. (**8**) Moreover, there would be a strong industrial lobby against it because of the extra costs and, thirdly, the government would be against it, as it would result in increased inflation. (**9**) So politicians would not support such a measure. (**10**) Nevertheless, I strongly believe that a carbon tax is an essential step in the fight against pollution.

On the opposite page are ten multiple choice questions with four alternatives.

Read the passage again and decide which alternatives best describe the purpose of each sentence and why the others are not suitable. In some cases, more than one alternative may be correct.

a book on **writing**

1. a. introducing the general subject of pollution
   b. a topic sentence
   c. a proposal
   d. an organising sentence

2. a. introducing the general subject of pollution
   b. a topic sentence
   c. a proposal
   d. an organising sentence

3. a. introducing the topic of the paragraph
   b. a proposal
   c. a tentative proposal
   d. expanding the word measures in sentence 2

4. a. a development of the previous sentence
   b. a conclusion
   c. a result
   d. a recommendation

5. a. a result
   b. an explanation of the organising word: benefits
   c. an expansion of the previous sentence
   d. a suggestion

6. a. a result
   b. an explanation of the organising word: benefits
   c. an expansion of the previous sentence
   d. a suggestion

7. a. a reservation
   b. a suggestion
   c. a result
   d. a contrast

8. a. a conclusion
   b. a recommendation
   c. a cause
   d. additional reservations and reasons

9. a. a tentative result
   b. an example
   c. a generalisation
   d. a conclusion of sentences 7 and 8

10. a. a contrast
    b. an opinion
    c. an example
    d. a conclusion for the whole paragraph

Exercise 8
Awareness of coherence in a paragraph

Below is the beginning of an essay. Read the text carefully and, while you are doing so, keep in mind what you learnt in the previous two exercises. Think specifically about the coherence in the text.

On the page opposite, there is a list of words and phrases to describe the purpose or function of each sentence. Study the list and decide which purpose or function describes each sentence. Note that a sentence may have more than one function.

Experiments on animals should be banned. What is your opinion?

(1) Experiments on animals may have contributed enormously to the welfare of the human race. (2) Nevertheless, I personally feel that such experiments are totally unacceptable for many reasons.

(3) By far the most important reason is the suffering that animals have to endure during tests. (4) Every year, many thousands of innocent creatures are used in laboratory experiments. (5) Cosmetics companies, for instance, test many of their products on rabbits and dogs to make sure they are safe for humans. (6) Such testing, however, means that harmless animals have to endure appalling pain and torture for the vanity of human beings. (7) Surely, the cosmetics industry should use other techniques now available, like computer models; or, instead, they could develop new methods. (8) The main counter argument is that a human life is more important than that of an animal. (9) Furthermore, the countless lives saved by animal experiments cannot be overlooked. (10) Still, in my opinion, experiments on animals do not justify the suffering caused to innocent creatures.

(11) Another argument against is that animals also have rights.

---

a book on **writing**

Function list

a. a conclusion

b. an expansion of the previous sentence

c. supplying background information

d. giving an example

e. an explanation

f. an argument against animal experiments

g. a topic sentence for the essay

h. an organising sentence

i. a concession

j. alternative solutions

k. suggestions

l. an opinion

m. an expansion of the word 'reasons'

n. introducing the general subject of the essay

o. an argument for animal experiments

p. a contrast

q. introducing the focus or topic of a paragraph

r. introducing a reason

Reminder

Write your answers on a separate sheet for all the exercises so that you can repeat
them.

Exercise 9
Organising a paragraph by questions

In this exercise, you are going to look at some of the thought processes involved in writing a text. Read the instructions below.

Instructions:

1. Imagine that you have to write an essay on the following title:

   All blood sports should be banned. Discuss the main arguments for this statement and then give your own opinion.

2. Imagine that you are writing the introduction and the first argument for the above essay title.

3. Imagine that the questions below are your own.

4. Read the questions one at a time.

5. Match each question with an answer from the jumbled text on the opposite page.

6. Answer the questions in sequence.

Three of the sentences opposite do not match any of the questions.

---

1. The first statement in the essay title above is written in such a way that it will create a discussion, and is, therefore, controversial. As a starting point, can I write a general statement about blood sports to include this idea?

2. How many arguments are there supporting a ban on blood sports?

3. What is the main reason for banning blood sports?

4. Can I give some background information about the numbers of helpless creatures killed for pleasure each year?

5. What do people think about blood sports? Are they barbaric/ uncivilised?

6. There must surely be many examples to support this view. Can I give one?

7. Can I explain this example more fully?

8. What does such cruelty do to people in general?

9. Can I draw a personal conclusion from this?

a book on **writing**

a. There are, however, many arguments for and against banning blood sports.

b. In this instance, an innocent animal is chased by men and women on horses and by a pack of dogs. When the poor creature is trapped, it is then inhumanely killed and may even be viciously torn to pieces by the dogs.

c. Consequently, people's tolerance of brutality is increased and other violent activities, including crime, are encouraged.

d. As far as I am concerned, sports are quite civilised.

e. There are, however, many reasons why blood sports should be made illegal.

f. Every year many thousands of helpless animals and birds are killed in this country, not primarily for food, but for pleasure.

g. Finally, blood sports cannot really be considered as sport at all and are a waste of time.

h. Fox-hunting is probably the best example of the sheer brutality of such entertainment.

i. For my part, after considering the arguments above, I feel there can be no justification whatsoever for allowing blood sports to continue.

j. Few issues arouse more bitter controversy than attempts to ban hunting animals for sport.

k. To many people, this practice is barbaric, because innocent animals are tortured and killed for the amusement and gratification of human beings.

l. The most obvious justification for the ban is that blood sports such as fox-hunting, shooting birds and, in fact, any form of game-hunting, are uncivilised.

Exercise 10
More questions for organising

Look at the text below and the list of jumbled questions which follow. Match each question to a sentence in the text.

The responsibility for reducing juvenile crime in the UK lies as much with parents and teachers as with the government. Discuss.

(**1**) Crime committed by young people in the UK is an ever-increasing problem. (**2**) Although there is some suggestion that the government should take the lead in reducing juvenile crime by, say, introducing more severe forms of punishment, parents and teachers certainly have a greater role to play in this process.

(**3**) Statistics show that young offenders frequently come from unstable, uncaring or violent family backgrounds. (**4**) A comfortable family environment is, therefore, one of the most important factors in helping to reduce crime committed by the young. (**5**) It is obviously the parents' responsibility to teach and bring up their children to follow the law and to behave as respected members of our society. (**6**) Of course, not every family can create the ideal surroundings for educating their children. (**7**) In that case, teachers could share the burden of teaching young people how and why they should obey rules. (**8**) The government, of course, also has a very important part to play. (**9**) It is surely the state's role to provide the environment necessary for a stable, caring society.

Questions

a. *Is it possible for all families to create an appropriate environment for their children?*

b. *Has the government any role to play? If so, how great?*

c. *What are the responsibilities of parents?*

d. *What is the government's role specifically?*

e. *What is the rate of juvenile crime in the United Kingdom at the moment?*

f. *What do the statistics say about juvenile crime in the UK?*

g. *If this is so, what is the most important factor in helping to reduce juvenile crime?*

h. *Who else could share the burden if parents cannot do it all themselves?*

i. *Which of the two groups, parents and teachers or the government, has the greater role to play?*

---

a book on **writing**

Exercise 11
Creating questions for organising a text

The text below is part of an essay written by a student. Read through the passage quickly. Then read it again, carefully, and decide what questions the writer asked himself to develop the essay. Write your questions, in full, on a piece of paper.

What would you do to improve the lot of the elderly in this country?

The UK, like other countries in Europe, has an increasingly ageing population, yet it is a pity that the elderly are not properly looked after or cared for. There are many ways, however, in which the lot of elderly people in this country can be improved.

The first step that needs to be taken is to improve the living conditions of all old people. According to statistics, there are over one million dwellings which have been declared unfit for habitation. Out of these, at least half a million are occupied by the elderly. Special houses should, therefore, be built, which are cheap, and designed in such a way that they are easily accessible. By this I mean, they ought to have special provision for those who have joint problems or difficulty in walking. Moreover, all the basic amenities should be nearby, so that the old will not have any trouble purchasing their food and other articles of daily use. The provision of adequate heating is a further improvement that could be made. These homes should be provided with proper heating facilities, as the elderly are susceptible to cold. It is estimated that hundreds of people who are old and frail die of hypothermia in their homes each winter.

Another area which requires attention is food.

Exercise 12
The sequence of tenses

Verbs also reflect and reinforce the relationships between sentences in a text.

In the passage below, choose the correct verb form from the alternatives given to fit the relationship between the sentences. Decide also why the other alternatives are not suitable.

Relations between different countries are now better than they have been for many years. Even so, there is a lot of tension in the world. What do you think governments should do to relieve this tension?

In my opinion, the tension in the world [1 *comes/is coming*] from ignorance and the lack of contact between different people and communities. To overcome this situation, there [2 *is/are/would be*] much that the international community can do. First of all, I [3 *am thinking/think*] governments [4 *should/would/might*] encourage their people, especially young people, to learn more languages. This [5 *would bring about/might bring about/brings about*] closer contact between different cultures and people. For example, at the moment many countries [6 *would give/will give/should give/give*] scholarships to enable people from other countries to study their languages. Most of these scholarships are for adults, but they [7 *would usefully be/could usefully be/are usefully*] extended to cover school children, or rather groups of school children.

Second, there [8 *could/would/might*] be more informal sporting events. For example, sports organisations in different countries [9 *could/would/might*] organise regional and international events on an amateur basis. Already, we [10 *are having/have/do have*] the Olympic Games, but, worthy though they are, they [11 *have become/would become/could become*] too political or too competitive. More informal sports meetings, however, in the true spirit of the Olympic Games [12 *would go/go*] some way to bringing people from all over the world together.

a book on **writing**

Exercise 13
Making choices

Read the following essay title:

> *Drug addiction among young people in the UK is daily becoming more and more serious. How, in your opinion, should the problem be tackled?*

Now read through the Maze below. At each number choose the correct sentence to develop the first paragraph of the above essay title. The sentences are in the correct order.

1. Drug addiction among the young in the UK is, unfortunately, on the increase.	
A	**B**
2. The problem, however, is not insurmountable, if it is approached realistically.	The problem, in my opinion, comes not just from the break-up of the family, but from other sources as well.
3. Peer group pressure is, I feel, one of the most likely causes of addiction among young people.	In my opinion, the most effective method to combat drug addiction among young people is through health education.
4. Such education can be divided roughly into two broad categories, namely health education in school and out of school.	What often happens here is that youngsters start playing around with drugs, because they see their friends taking them.
5. At school, children and teenagers can be shown the dangers of drug addiction in health education classes.	They do not want to be left out or, as is frequently the case, taking drugs becomes a kind of badge of acceptance within a group.
6. Then, if someone does not do what the others in the group are doing, they may be ostracised or cut off by their friends.	The older pupils could do projects on addiction; watch videos on the topic; speak to ex-addicts, and so on.
7. Education outside the school could take the form of advertising on television and the radio, as well as in magazines aimed at young people.	All one has to do is to look at the prevalence of smoking among youngsters to realise the extent of the danger from such pressure.
8. The advertisers could use well-known figures that young people admire, and are likely to listen to, like pop stars and footballers.	Money is another cause of addiction.
9. Nowadays, the younger generation have more pocket money and are able to earn quite a bit from part-time jobs.	In this way, drug addiction would then be prevented before it starts.
10. Thus, when something novel like drugs comes their way, they can often afford to try it out, at least once.	

In Roger's English class recently, he and his fellow students had a lively discussion about whether intelligence is inherited or not. During the debate, Roger supported the opinion that it is impossible to separate the inheritance from the environmental factors when discussing intelligence.

One student in the pro-inheritance group raised the point that there are many examples of people who are very gifted and who rise to the top no matter what happens. This was an argument which Roger's group could not disagree with.

Roger, however, also raised the point that there are many talented people, but, without the right environment and influences, they are held back. He then observed that intelligent parents tend to encourage their children and provide an environment favourable to development.

He went on to quote examples of families where the parents are not considered generally to be 'bright', yet their children are top of the class at school. Conversely, as he also mentioned, there are students who are not very good academically, but whose parents are both in intellectually demanding professions.

At the end of the lesson, the teacher asked the class to express their views in an essay entitled:

Is intelligence inherited?

Bearing in mind the opinion of Roger's group, choose sentences opposite that would make up the first paragraph of his essay. You may use only eight of the sentences to reflect the points above. Text number 14 is the third sentence which Roger wrote.

a book on **writing**

1. All this leads me to conclude that the interplay between environmental and hereditary factors is crucial in the development of human intelligence.

2. Intelligence is very difficult to measure, but, if we look at the issue carefully, we can identify certain criteria for assessment.

3. In other words, intelligent parents mean intelligent children.

4. Nevertheless, there are countless others who are talented, but without the right environment and influences they do not realise their full potential.

5. For example, most professional families produce children who are very successful and follow a professional career.

6. Further, surely parents who are intelligent and are successful are more likely to try to provide an environment which nurtures the development of their children.

7. Looking at the issue from another angle, there are many intelligent children who do not have intelligent parents, and vice versa.

8. This gives rise to the statement that doctors are born, not made.

9. Some people rightly feel that intelligence depends solely on hereditary factors.

10. I accept that there are some people who are very talented and they succeed no matter what happens.

11. However, I personally believe that intelligence is based on a mixture of both hereditary and environmental factors.

12. An example of this is families where the parents and children are doctors.

13. The debate about whether intelligence is inherited has been raging for quite some time.

14. In fact, these factors are so inextricably interlinked that it is impossible to separate them.

15. In other words, they believe that people in certain professions, like musicians, teachers, doctors, etc., are born, not made.

SECTION 2

Contents

a book on **writing**

Exercise 15
Sentence relationships – knowledge check 1

As you are writing, it is worth bearing in mind that it helps your readers if they can see clearly the relationship between your sentences. Quite often you can show this relationship with particular joining words or phrases. Not only are you then guiding the reader through your thoughts in written form, but you are also directing yourself.

In this exercise, you are going to test how much you know about some basic connecting devices, or text markers.

Answer the questions below as far as you can. Do not expect to know all the answers. One aim of this exercise is to help you check and then organise your knowledge.

Avoid writing in the book so that you can do the exercise several times, if necessary.

1. To connect sentences you can use basically two types of connecting words or phrases: **adverbs** and **conjunctions**. In the list below, which words are adverbs and which conjunctions?

   while, and, besides, consequently, moreover, although, if, where, when, but, however, though, thus, what is more.

2. What is the difference between an adverb which links sentences and a conjunction?

3. Which of the two sentences below is correct?

   (a) *The steps that have been taken are admirable, but they may be too late to do any good.*

   (b) *The steps that have been taken are admirable, however they may be too late to do any good.*

4. Is the text below correct?

   The steps that have been taken are admirable.
   But they may be too late to do any good.

5. What is the difference between <u>although</u> and <u>but</u>?

6. What is the difference between <u>yet</u> and <u>but</u>?

7. In the list below which word or phrase is the odd one out?

   similarly, furthermore, on the other hand, moreover, in addition, what is more.

8. When can you use <u>much as</u> to link sentences together?

9. Which is the odd one out:

   such as, like, namely, for example?

10. There is a problem in the text below. What is it?

    Take rugby, for example, it is also a sport which can cause considerable injury.

a book on **writing**

Exercise 16
Sentence relationships – knowledge check 2

This exercise is also a test of your knowledge of basic text markers, which help to lead both you and the reader through your writing.

Answer the questions below as far as you can. Again, do not expect to know all the answers; the exercise is to help you check and organise your knowledge.

Avoid writing in the book so that you can do the exercise several times, if necessary.

1. *It's not easy to deal with a situation like this. It's a bit much, though, to put all this pressure on your friends.*
   Is the word <u>though</u> in the second sentence an adverb or a conjunction?

2. Explain the connection between the three sentences below. The third sentence is also unfinished; fill the gap with one word.

   A man appeared round the corner and walked briskly along the street. The man stopped suddenly and was about to enter a shop. _____ door was open, and so ....

3. The text below is not well connected. Where does the problem lie and can you correct it?

   Another reason why is that alcohol advertisements are responsible for a large number of health problems. In fact, alcohol advertisements cause millions of deaths in any one year.

4. Use the texts below to explain the difference between <u>in the end</u> and <u>finally</u>.

   (a) *At first, she was useless at driving, but, in the end, she became a very good driver.*

   (b) *First, he bought all the decorating equipment he needed. Next, he washed down the walls and, then, he painted them. Finally, he cleared up the mess.*

   (c) *First, read all the questions very carefully. Second, check how many questions you have to answer; and, finally, write only the number of words required.*

5. What do the following words and phrases have in common:

   so/therefore/as a result/as a consequence/accordingly/consequently/ now/then/because of this/that/thus/hence/for this/that reason

6. Look at the sentences below. In which sentence is the use of <u>otherwise</u> correct?

   (a) *This matter needs to be examined carefully; otherwise, there will be problems in the future.*

   (b) *This matter needs to be examined carefully, otherwise there will be problems in the future.*

7. What is the difference between <u>despite</u> and <u>in spite of</u> and <u>although</u>. Join the two sentences below to show the difference.

   He played a major role in the peace process. His achievement went unrecognised.

8. *There are a lot of measures can be introduced to remedy the situation.* What is wrong with this sentence?

9. What is the difference between <u>first</u> and <u>at first</u>?

10. In the extract below, the word <u>Another</u> tells you that this is the second subject under discussion. Which noun or nouns can you put in the space below?

   Another delicate _____ needs to be considered here: at what age children should be given information about sex. To many people, giving such information at an early age is much too dangerous.

Exercise 17
Some areas of confusion

From the last two exercises, you have probably realised that you do, in fact, know most connecting words and phrases. However, you may have discovered that there is often some vital information, about even very common connecting devices, of which you are not aware. So, when it comes to putting these linking words into a text, you may find it difficult to use them correctly.

This exercise looks at a few areas where students are sometimes confused. In each pair of sentences below, one sentence is correct and the other is wrong. Decide which answer is correct and why.

1a. The government tightened the laws on censorship, because the media could be brought under stricter control.	1b. So that the media could be brought under stricter control, the government tightened the laws on censorship.

        a book on **writing**

2a. The arguments for restrictions on gun ownership are, as we have seen, overwhelming. Therefore, the law should be changed.

2b. The arguments for restrictions on gun ownership are, as we have seen, overwhelming, therefore, the law should be changed.

3a. Although you have been expressly forbidden to leave before 3 pm, yet you continue to do so.

3b. Although you have been expressly forbidden to leave before 3 pm, but you continue to do so.

4a. Planting trees in cities will make the environment more pleasant to live in. Beside, it will make the air cleaner as well.

4b. Planting trees in cities will make the environment more pleasant to live in. Besides, it will make the air cleaner as well.

5a. Many improvements have been made to the infrastructure. Even so, more has yet to be done.

5b. Many improvements have been made to the infrastructure, even so more has yet to be done.

6a. Jane and Diva got up early so they would be able to catch the first train.

6b. Jane and Diva got up early, so they would be able to catch the first train.

7a. Although the talks on nuclear disarmament were successful, we can now look forward to a more relaxed world.

7b. Because the talks on nuclear disarmament were successful, we can now look forward to a more relaxed world.

8a. Much as I sympathise with this position, I cannot accept that euthanasia is really the answer.

8b. Even I sympathise with this position, I cannot accept that euthanasia is really the answer.

9a. There are four main skills in language learning, like, speaking, listening, reading and writing.

9b. There are four main skills in language learning, namely: speaking, listening, reading and writing.

10a. Some people, namely Aristotle, Leonardo da Vinci and Einstein, have contributed much to the development of mankind.

10b. Some people, like Aristotle, Leonardo da Vinci and Einstein, have contributed much to the development of mankind.

11a. He had driven all night, so he was tired.

11b. He had driven all night, therefore he was tired.

Exercise 18
Split texts

Now you are going to look at connections in another way. Match the text on the left with a suitable clause or sentence on the right.

As you do the exercise, think about the relationship between the two parts of the text.

1.	Despite the fact that he arrived in this country as a penniless refugee,	a.	that thousands of people fled from the area.
2.	The outbreak of the disease caused such a panic,	b.	that he won the Nobel Prize for Physics.
3.	Now that more and more people have access to the Internet,	c.	Nevertheless, I cannot bear him personally.
4.	The roads were jammed,	d.	he was finally arrested and sent to prison.
5.	Being a competent linguist,	e.	they will be able to find their way here quite easily.
6.	There is no doubt that the law needs to be changed	f.	she is able to understand the problems that her students face.
7.	I admire him as a politician.	g.	so that people with physical disabilities can have greater access to all public buildings.
8.	It was such a brilliant development,	h.	the number of injuries would have been dramatically reduced.
9.	On account of his violent behaviour towards his wife and children,	i.	yet the ambulance managed to reach the scene of the accident.
10.	Had the wearing of safety belts been compulsory on coaches as well as in cars,	j.	he has managed to overcome all his difficulties.
11.	In the end, he bought the building,	k.	the amount of information moving around the globe is phenomenal.
12.	Something needs to be done about water conservation in many parts of the world;	l.	otherwise, there may well be wars in the near future.
13.	Provided they follow the instructions,	m.	even though it was practically falling down.

a book on **writing**

Exercise 19
Lost connecting words and phrases

In the sentences below, the connecting words and phrases are missing. Read through the exercise first and see if you can identify where you need to add an appropriate connector. The punctuation will help you to decide what you need and where. Note that you can only use connectors which the punctuation allows. Sometimes, you may be able to use more than one item to connect the sentences.

Use only words and phrases from the list below the exercise. If, however, you feel confident enough, try to do the exercise without using the list.

Example:

In sentence 1, you have to put a connecting word at the beginning of the sentence, because <u>he</u> has a small letter. You can use <u>When</u>, <u>Once</u> or <u>As soon as</u>.

---

1.   he had found the key, he was able to get out.

2.   action had been taken sooner, this tragedy would not have occurred.

3.   the exams are over, I can relax.

4.   There are many things you can do to get exercise, walking, swimming, cycling, tennis and so on.

5.   a referee sees that a boxer is hurt, he should stop the fight.

6.   television has had a detrimental effect on society, it has brought many benefits.

7.   There are many steps can be taken to make public transport safer.

8.   the law on gun ownership in the UK should be more strictly controlled is now being seriously considered.

9.   the leak is mended, the structure of the house will be severely damaged.

10.   They ate their meal quickly and left the restaurant the owner could close early.

11.   Maureen teaches botany Violet teaches history.

12.   the number of car accidents is decreasing in the UK, in other countries, it is increasing.

13.   The plane was delayed; the hotel was a mess and it rained most of the time; the holiday was a disaster.

14.   the violence occurred rarely. Then over the years it became worse.

Item bank

if/unless/when/if only/like/so that/and/whether/that/at first/whereas/but/ although/however/all in all/now that/since/which/as soon as/once

---

This exercise will help you focus on marking the relationships between sentences in a text. Obviously, highlighting such connections is much more complex than just joining a few sentences or clauses together.

First of all, read the introduction and the first paragraph of the essay below. As you are reading, try to feel where there is a need for connecting devices to mark the sentence relationships in the passage.

Then, use the guidelines which follow the text and write out the passage, connecting the sentences where possible.

Avoid marking the book.

What are the arguments for and against private vehicles? What is your opinion in this matter?

(**1**) Private vehicles play a key role in our lives. (**2**) They provide independent transport, freedom and many jobs. (**3**) They cause pollution, traffic jams, noise and death.

(**4**) Private transport, especially the car, gives us freedom to move. (**5**) We no longer need to organise our lives around bus or train timetables. (**6**) Many people think that their cars are indispensable machines. (**7**) They cannot live without them. (**8**) People who live in rural areas need private vehicles to go to towns for shopping, socialising, taking children to schools, etc. (**9**) Without a car their lives would be very difficult. (**10**) They would be forced to rely on infrequent public transport, if it existed at all. (**11**) Many families who live in the country have one or more cars. (**12**) They would be cut off from the rest of the world. (**13**) For many people a car is a necessity.

---

a book on **writing**

Guidelines for sentence relationships

<u>Sentences 1 and 2</u>. You can join these sentences together; the second sentence states the reasons why such vehicles play an important role.

<u>Sentence 3</u> shows the opposite side of the picture, so insert an adverb that brings out the contrast. Be careful with the punctuation! You will find in the Key that the author has added another phrase, because he finds that the contrast is not strong enough, and because there is a problem with the rhythm of the sentence. Can you add something yourself to the sentence?

<u>Sentence 4</u> is the first argument of your essay. Add a word or phrase to indicate this.

<u>Sentence 5</u> is a consequence of <u>Sentence 4</u>. Use a conjunction to join them together.

<u>Sentence 6</u> is an extension of the previous one. It states another true fact about private vehicles. Can you add a phrase to help show this?

<u>Sentence 7</u> is a result of <u>Sentence 6</u>.

<u>Sentence 8</u> is an example of the previous sentence.

You can join <u>Sentences 9 and 10</u> with a simple conjunction that indicates the two are of the same value.

<u>Sentence 11</u> is a consequence.

Can you think of an adverb to join <u>Sentence 12</u> to the previous one? Use a word that means <u>or else</u>. Be careful with the punctuation.

<u>Sentence 13</u> is a conclusion.

Exercise 21
Text with gaps

You are now going to connect the sentences in a text by inserting suitable words and phrases, but, this time, you will have no help.

A. Look at the items in the following list:

1. Further
2. and consequently AIDS
3. Take the threat of AIDS, for example
4. In my opinion
5. especially young girls
6. First of all, I believe
7. To me, however
8. To put it another way
9. Thirdly
10. Admittedly
11. whether sex education should be introduced
12. Even so, I strongly believe that it needs
13. What is more

Now read the passage below and write the numbers of the items from the list in the appropriate blanks. You may use each item once only.

B. What is the title of the essay?

The issue of ____(a)_____ in all schools at secondary level has been an on-going debate for quite some time. _____(b)_____, such education is a necessary part of the curriculum at this level.

_____(c)____ pupils need be given lessons on sex education, just like any other field of study. _____(d)_____, they should not be protected from this subject, as it is one of the most important matters in our everyday life. _____(e)____. Sex education would go a long way in preventing the spread of the HIV virus, ____(f)___, among the younger generation. _____(g)_____, there may be some reticence, and even antagonism, among certain groups of people, as to the way and the degree this subject is presented. _____(h)_____ to be part of the curriculum.

_____(i)_____, we have to remember what other hazards ignorance about sex may bring for pupils, at secondary school, _____(j)_____. _____ (k)_____, it is better to know everything about this 'taboo' subject than to seek knowledge when it is too late, for example in the case of unwanted pregnancies.

_____(l)_____, we all know that young people are especially vulnerable to stress as regards sex. Proper education would, I feel, help to prevent frustration in certain circumstances. _____(m)_____, it may also stop young people from seeking 'nonscientific' ways of solving their problems, and halt the development of superstition.

As we can see, there are many arguments to support giving lessons in sex education at secondary school.

---

a book on **writing**

Exercise 22
Text with no gaps

From Exercises 15 to 21, you have been concentrating on connecting words and phrases which contribute to the texture of what you write. This exercise attempts to focus your attention more on this quality to help you improve your writing. Below are the introduction and first two paragraphs of an essay on _Knowledge is power. Discuss_. The text is grammatically correct, but it is not well connected. Put the numbers which relate to the words and phrases below into the most appropriate place in the text, as in the two examples. The punctuation will help you to complete the exercise. If you are not able to put in all the words and phrases in the first few attempts, use the Key to help you.

1. Work is another obvious area where knowledge bestows power.
2. In a similar way,
3. For example,
4. In fact, in all areas of life,
5. Looking at the matter from another angle,
6. above
7. When the successful candidate finally starts working,
8. , thus,
9. so that
10. A very good example is the field of politics.
11. At the interview itself,
12. , for instance,
13. are then more likely to
14. With this power,
15. This
16. such as
17. , among other things,

Few people would deny the validity of the __6__ saying. the power of knowledge exerts a considerable force.

As some politicians have access to many sources of information, they possess a formidable weapon: power. they are able to control the lives of the general public. when politicians want public support for a particular cause, all they have to do is put forward the positive aspects of their proposals and hide the negative. The public, ignorant of the whole picture, lend their support to the politicians' cause. other politicians are also controlled. the general public and other politicians, through lack of knowledge, are at the mercy of the politician who possesses knowledge, and power.

When someone applies for a job __12__ the success of the application depends on the knowledge of the person who applies. knowledge involves skills, knowing how best to complete the application form; using the correct language; or how to write the accompanying letter. the success of the application will depend on the applicant's display of knowledge about the post applied for. success or failure will largely be dependent on his/her accumulation of knowledge, he/she can deal effectively with others and not be manipulated by them, too much.

Check your answers with the Key and correct any of the numbers. Then read the text to yourself and try to put in the words and phrases above automatically. Repeat the exercise several times so that you can learn to feel where there is a gap in the text.

Exercise 23
Reference with synonyms

The use of synonyms to link sentences also improves the quality and texture of a passage. When you are writing, synonyms help you summarise part of the previous text, and, thus, link sentences together. Furthermore, they help you to avoid repetition and stop you from relying over much on adverbs and conjunctions to make connections.

Below is a list of such words that are often used to help link sentences. Put the words into the appropriate spaces below. Note that in some cases it is possible to use more than one word. You may also be able to think of other words from outside the list.

solution/ entertainment/ problem/ proposal/ policy/ group/ violence/ measure/ move/
idea/ situation/ ploy/ amenities/ recommendation/ fact/ suggestion/ crime/ damage

Try not to write the answers in your book. When you have compared your answers with the Key, repeat the exercise over a period of time until the words come automatically.

---

1. Old people should be given a higher pension during winter months. This seems to be the best possible _____ to the problem.

2. Millions of people are dying each year because of a lack of basic medicine; a _____ that surely cannot be ignored.

3. Many inner cities have been disfigured by insensitive office developments, but the _____, I feel, is not irreparable.

4. Safety belts should be made compulsory on all coaches. If this _____ were adopted, it would certainly help reduce injuries in road accidents.

5. More swimming pools, leisure centres and sports clubs are being built all over the country. Even so, there are still not enough _____ like this to satisfy demand.

6. Scenes of murder and physical assault are now commonplace on TV. Such _____, unfortunately, has a negative effect on the minds of young people.

7. The Department of Transport has decided to introduce a green tax on fuel. There are, of course, many people who would object to the introduction of this _____.

8. Making petty criminals wear electronic tags has been a failure in the United States. Surprisingly, the _____ is being considered by the Home Office in the UK.

9. Young people nowadays have many forms of technology to amuse them. Teachers often disapprove of such _____, as it tends to make students lazy and unable to think for themselves.

10. Society often fails to meet the needs of physically handicapped people. Yet they are a _____ that obviously deserves more help.

11. The government introduced the new rule while everyone's attention was engaged elsewhere. It was quite a clever _____.

---

a book on **writing**

Exercise 24
More reference with synonyms

This exercise gives you further practice with synonyms. Read the sentences below and think of a suitable word for each of the blanks. Note that in some cases it is possible to use more than one word. Only this time, try to do the exercise without any help, if you can.

As you read, try to predict which words will be translated into a synonym in the next part of the text. Then as you choose each synonym think about the text which it looks back to. Let us take an example from the previous exercise:

  6. a   <u>Scenes of murder and physical assault</u> are now commonplace on TV.

      b   Such <u>entertainment/violence</u>, unfortunately, has a negative effect on the minds of young people.

In (a), the underlined text looks forward to both the synonyms in (b). The synonyms, in turn, look back to the text underlined in (a).

If you cannot find a word which fits, then select one from the list on the next page.

  1. Animals are kept in appalling conditions during transport from one country to another. Surely, _____ of this kind cannot be tolerated in a civilised society.

  2. Violent attacks by young people are increasing alarmingly, but little is being done to address the _____.

  3. Poverty and ill-health are inextricably bound together, yet the _____ between them does not appear to be recognised by those in power.

  4. In 1945, there were 100,000 vegetarians in the United Kingdom and now there are 3 million. With 2000 people changing to a meat-free diet each week, it is a _____ that is set to continue.

  5. Euthanasia may have to be considered as a possible solution to overpopulation in the future; at the moment, fortunately, it is not a serious _____.

  6. One way to solve the problem would be to legalise the use of cannabis and other soft drugs. This _____ could, of course, prove to be rather risky.

  7. He said that I should have taken up the job. If I had followed his _____, though, I would have been completely worn out by now.

  8. Through the media, people are now being encouraged to recycle different materials like bottles, paper. plastic bags, etc. Such _____ doesn't always work.

  9. The Project can only go ahead, if 75% of the funding is found from the private sector. In the present climate such a _____ will be difficult to fulfil.

  10. If speed limits on motorways were reduced, the number of car accidents would fall dramatically. This is obviously a highly desirable _____.

  11. The world is in imminent danger of being destroyed by the greenhouse effect. Yet little is being done to counter this _____.

  12. With the rising costs of medicine, the question of whether to allocate scarce resources to the elderly or the young is a _____ many hospitals now face.

Below is a list of words you can use to help link the sentences on the previous page.

disaster, outcome, dilemma, craze, action, advice, issue, danger, relationship, encouragement, problem, cruelty, threat, trend, link, step, condition, situation, connection, practices, option, policy, predicament, treatment, catastrophe, requirement.

Exercise 25
Words and phrases that are not exactly correct

When you are writing, it is difficult to think about the grammar and spelling as well as the different connecting devices, all at the same time. However, if you can learn to control the reference and connections in your writing, it gives you greater freedom, and more time, to concentrate on the content and the ideas.

In this exercise, you are going to look at a mixture of connections. Some words or phrases are almost correct; some are completely wrong; and yet others are repetitions. Read the text below once and then read it again, replacing, where possible, the underlined words with suitable words/phrases. Try not to mark the text so that you can repeat the exercise.

Why are people turning more and more to alternative medicine?

Alternative, or non-orthodox, medicine is now attracting an ever-increasing number of people. There are, **(1) however**, many **(2) causes** behind this **(3) custom**.

The most important argument is the public's increased awareness of their **(4) condition**. **(5) The public** are no longer willing to bear the mildest of pain, **(6) as** headaches, or **(7) bear** even minor illnesses like flu. **(8) On the other hand**, **(9) the public** spare no effort looking for help by any means available. As orthodox medicine often does not work or needs time to work, **(10) they** do not hesitate to seek help from an acupuncturist or osteopath in the hope of better relief. **(11) And** in chronic situations, **(12) namely** arthritis, headaches or backache, where **(13) orthodox medicine** can often do little, some forms of **(14) unorthodox medicine** are favoured by an increasing number of people.

(15) Other important reason is that **(16) in contrary** to orthodox medicine, non-orthodox forms of treatment do not usually involve much intervention. **(17) They** also fear being admitted to hospital for any length of time, taking drugs or chemicals, which may do harm. Above all, they **(18) fear** operations of any kind. **(19) In addition**, when something simple promises relief, they naturally **(20) switch** to it.

a book on **writing**

Exercise 26
The definite article as a connecting word

You have looked at joining sentences together by various means. It is now time to focus on another linking device, the definite article.

In the exercise below, explain the use of the articles, the/a/an, and the lack of articles, as far as you can. Then read the Key carefully. You may need to do the exercise several times.

1. A man was walking slowly along a dark street of low cottages. The street was narrow and unwelcoming. As he glanced into the alleys between some of the cottages, the man looked quite scared.

2. The advice you gave me was unsound.

3. The blind may benefit from new developments in technology.

4. The walk to Studland along the beach from the ferry takes just over an hour.

5. I usually hear from him twice a year.

6. We were sitting in an old café. The sun was shining in a blue sky, but it was bitterly cold. The room was very cosy and the hot chocolate was warm and rich.

7. Islands are romantic places and the Seychelles are no exception.

8. The most important bee in a hive is the queen.

9. In the following exercise fill the blanks with a suitable word.

10. I was set upon from behind. The attack lasted only about five minutes, but, believe me, it seemed like a very long time.

Exercise 27
The articles: fill the gaps

Now you have a chance to use the information you learnt in the previous exercise to complete a series of texts. For each blank in the texts below, decide whether you should add either a/an/the, or leave the space empty. Remember to ask yourself the questions you learnt in the Key in the previous exercise. Again try not to mark the text so that you can repeat the exercise.

___1___ advice is often difficult to accept from ___2___ friends, but ___3___ advice Samir gave me was surprisingly helpful. The next time I need ___4___ help I shall know where to go.

___5___ old people always think that ___6___ young lack ___7___ discipline; maybe it's because ___8___ young people are free from ___9___ shackles that hindered ___10___ previous generations.

___11___ first time she saw him she was only thirteen. His curly auburn hair and sailor's uniform were what did it. ___12___ year later she was out delivering ___13___ milk on her bicycle, when she saw him for ___14___ second time. He was also on ___15___ bike. If you are going in ___16___ opposite directions, ___17___ bicycles are not very convenient for starting ___18___ love affair!

___19___ whales are in ___20___ danger of becoming extinct.

___21___ rubbish left by ___22___ climbers on ___23___ Himalayas is building up.

Sarah and Matty were ___24___ great friends. Whenever Sarah went out to see her at ___25___ big house, Matty would always make her tea in ___26___ large kitchen. Then, if Lady Margaret were not around, they would slide down ___27___ banisters on ___28___ staircase in ___29___ front entrance hall. How difficult it is, when you are young, to resist ___30___ banisters, especially if they look dangerous!

On ___31___ arrival at ___32___ airport, ___33___ first thing he did was phone home.

___34___ Giant's Causeway is one of ___35___ most beautiful places in ___36___ Europe.

a book on **writing**

Exercise 28
Reference awareness and connections in a text

Below is part of an article for a school magazine on: *Life in 100 years' time; a personal view.*
Read the text through carefully; you will see that the passage is not very well connected.

Just as it would have been difficult to predict, a hundred years ago, life in this century, so now it is not easy to say what life is going to be like in 100 years' time.

First of all, I must say that I think life will be very different in many ways by the year 2096. People will be living on other planets, perhaps even on planets outside the solar system. Obviously, therefore, travelling will be incredibly sophisticated and people will be able to travel vast distances in space; perhaps, even in a matter of seconds.

Secondly, communication is also bound to be so sophisticated, that people will be able to communicate by telepathy. Another possibility is that people may be able to communicate visually with each other wherever they are. For example, people will be able to send holographic messages to each other; these holographic messages will be able to be stored for play back later, just as answering machines do today.

Thirdly, a planet is certain to be free from disease and, as a consequence, we will have a longer lifespan. Many people may fear the introduction of euthanasia as the earth becomes more crowded, but, if it is introduced, I believe that it will be only a temporary measure, as more and more men and women will be needed to colonise other worlds.

Now try to improve the article by completing the following exercise:

1. The writer has repeated certain words and phrases. Use the synonyms below, in the order they occur in the list, to improve the text.

    (a) the major events that have taken place; (b) our lives; (c) worlds; (d) cover; (e) highly developed; (f) we; (g) everyone; (h) human beings; (i) one another; (j) images;

    For example, **(c)** worlds = planets in Paragraph 2.

2. Are the words and phrases below necessary in the text?

    First of all, in many ways, Secondly, Thirdly, For example, as a consequence,

3. The writer couldn't decide whether to add , therefore, to the beginning of the second sentence in the fourth paragraph. In your opinion, is it necessary?

4. In one place in the fourth paragraph, the indefinite article a is used instead of the? Why is it wrong?

5. Note also that the writer has repeated the structure will be able to four times. What other alternatives can you use in the third paragraph?

6. Which other two structures does the writer use to avoid the repetition of the construction will be?

Exercise 29
Awareness of old/new information in a sentence: 1

This exercise helps make you aware of the organisation of the information in a sentence.

Below is part of an article entitled *Violence in our Society*. The sentences of the first paragraph are divided into two parts. The part on the left is in the correct order, but the part on the right is jumbled.

Match the two sections and you will have a complete paragraph. As you do the exercise, think about the balance of the information in each sentence.

1. One of the most pressing problems	a. is the inability of society to tackle the root of the problem, namely poverty.
2. This increase can be attributed	b. operate in isolation.
3. Lack of discipline in the home and at school	c. to many different causes depending on one's particular viewpoint.
4. The break-up of marriages and the increase in one-parent families	d. is often quoted as a reason for the disintegration of our society.
5. But without doubt the primary cause	e. are also blamed for the increasing violence in our lives.
6. Poverty is often the source of a host of other contributory factors,	f. like the lack of opportunity, squalor and unemployment, to name but a few.
7. However, rarely does one of the above causes	g. facing our society today is the increasing incidence of violence.

Exercise 30
Awareness of old/new information in a sentence: 2

This exercise helps you to focus on the organisation of the information in a sentence from a different angle. Below is part of an essay: *Inequalities in health care cannot be avoided. Discuss.* The sentences of the second paragraph are divided into two. The parts indicated by letters, which contain the text references, are jumbled, but those indicated by numbers, containing the ideas, are in the correct order. Match the two sections of each sentence and you will have a complete paragraph.

Read through the part of the text on the opposite page carefully. Use the connecting words and phrases, the grammar and the sequence of information, to help you find your way through the text.

As you do the exercise think about the relationship between the two parts of each sentence and how they connect.

a book on **writing**

Introduction

Not all people in the world enjoy equal standards of health care, simply because not everyone in the world has equal access to such care.

Second paragraph

a. This treatment is available, because there are

b. In the latter, however, there are

c. First of all, the rich can afford to go to

d. What is more, those living in

e. Second, for people living in big cities it is

f. Thus, for poor people living in remote areas

g. Poor patients, on the other hand, have to go to

---

1. a private hospital where they are able to have better investigations and treatment without delay.

2. a government hospital where they may encounter many difficulties, including long waiting lists for treatment, or even a lack of basic supplies like bandages.

3. easier to find modern treatment.

4. many highly equipped hospitals available in large cities compared with small towns.

5. often no hospitals at all and public transport is non-existent.

6. large urban areas have access to more specialists in different fields with modern technology like CT scans, dialysis machines, etc.

7. access to health care is not easily available.

Exercise 31
Contradictions

As we have seen, it is difficult to think about the content, as well as the grammar and the connections, when we write. It is not surprising, therefore, that we sometimes contradict ourselves in minor detail.

Read through the text below quickly. Then read it again carefully and find the contradictions. Note that the first fact in the text is always true. One of the contradictions is marked for you.

<blockquote>

<u>Kimberley was born in 1953</u> and brought up in Hackney, north London, the only girl in a family of four boys. She had a happy childhood with parents who were very caring and easygoing. Being rather well-off, the family lived a totally carefree life in a large, rambling house.

5   Kimberley was quite an ordinary child, rather dull, in fact, with no real interest in any school activity. She was very mischievous and always getting into trouble. Her behaviour caused her parents no end of anguish, as her other brothers and sister were doing extremely well. At school, insects, drawing and, of course, boys were her main obsessions.

10   Then, in 1972, <u>at the age of sixteen</u>, Kimberley began to blossom. The plain girl turned into a very handsome young woman, but still very much a loner. She wasn't exactly elegant, as, coming from a poor background, she could not afford to buy many expensive clothes.

She had always been a model pupil of average intelligence, but now she began 15 to shine in the class, especially in languages. In her first attempt at her A-Levels, she did rather well, much to everyone's surprise.

Kim, as she was known to her many friends, couldn't decide whether to stay in south London, where she was born, or go to Exeter. She went to the latter, where she studied French and Italian. She lasted only two years, as she hated 20 the student life in London. As part of her course, she spent a year abroad: six months in Moscow and six in Athens. When she came back to England, she found it very difficult to settle down. Being decisive, at first, she didn't know what to do, but gradually Kimberley found her feet.

She started an acting career, which took off rather quickly. After a 25 considerable time, she had a lucky break in a comedy called *Right Monkey*, about a family who bring up a baby chimpanzee. The film was a huge success. She is now also a big hit in a romantic comedy, called *Hello and Bye*.

</blockquote>

a book on **writing**

Section 3

a book on **writing**

Contents

a book on **writing**

Exercise 32
Formal letter checklist Part 1

This exercise checks how much you know about formal letters. Read the statements below and decide whether they are true or false.

1. You can put your name above your address in the top right-hand corner.

2. You must never leave out punctuation in your address.

3. The date should always be immediately below your address.

4. You can abbreviate the date as follows: 22.8.96.

5. Quoting the reference of the person you are writing to is essential.

6. It is always necessary to put the name and the address of the addressee on the left, starting below your own address.

7. You must always give the position of the person you are writing to after his/her name in the address, e.g.:

   Mr Singh
   The Manager

8. If you do not know the addressee personally, but you know his/her name, you should still use Dear Sir/Madam to begin your letter.

9. All formal letters should begin with a heading on the line below Dear ....

10. You must always indent the beginning of each paragraph as follows:

    Dear Sir/Madam,

    I should like to apply .....

11. You should start a formal letter by stating why you are writing, e.g.:

    I am writing to complain about/apply for ...

    I should/would like to apply for the job ...

    Thank you for your letter dated ...

    I refer to your letter of ...

a book on **writing**

Exercise 33
Formal letter checklist Part 2

This is another exercise to check how much you know about formal letters. Read the statements below and decide whether they are true or false.

1. In the following sentence, you can use <u>would</u> instead of <u>should</u>:
    I should be grateful if you could send me a copy of the report.

2. When you are applying for a job, it is better to include a summary of your *curriculum vitae* in the letter.

3. You cannot use contractions (e.g. don't/I'm/can't).

4. <u>Hope to hear from you soon</u> is a good way to end a formal letter.

5. <u>Yours faithfully,</u> is used in all formal letters.

6. You should always say <u>Thank you/Thanking you in advance</u> at the end of formal letters.

7. It is better to print your name after your signature at the end of the letter.

8. You should avoid colloquial expressions, e.g. phrasal verbs, get, etc.

9. You do not need to write numbers in words.

10. When you use abbreviations in a formal letter, you should write the words in full with the abbreviation in brackets afterwards, e.g. the <u>United Kingdom</u> (<u>UK</u>). When you want to use the phrase/name again in the text, you can use the abbreviation on its own.

11. Formal letters should be fairly neat and tidy.

12. You must always use unlined paper.

Exercise 34
Formal letter analysis

In the letter below, there are a number of problems, which relate to style and layout. Edit the letter using the true/false checklists in Exercise 32 and 33.

27 Silver Street
London,
SE16 1CH
12/7/96.

Dear Sir

I'm a social worker living in London. Normally, I don't write to papers, but I feel I must do so on this occasion.

I must say that I don't agree with the writer's point of view. She has said that, with the use of fetal material for transplants, we are actively encouraging more abortions. A recent study, though, shows that about 175,000 abortions are carried out legally every year in the UK, which means that tissue from 175,000 fetal brains is available for transplantation. Do we then really need more abortions?

By carrying out these operations, we are helping loads of patients suffering from Parkinson's disease. (There are about 110,000 patients suffering from this condition in the UK). Thus, we can help a large number of people lead better and purposeful lives. Secondly, after the operation the patient has to take fewer drugs. Both these factors would reduce the load on the NHS as millions of pounds are spent on the rehabilitation of patients suffering from Parkinson's disease.

Finally, by stopping these operations we are actually trying to halt medical research and progress. How then can we hope to keep up with other developed nations where scientific progress is advancing at an incredible pace?

Hope I can get this letter published in your paper.

Yours sincerely,

a book on **writing**

Exercise 35
Sequence of tenses in a text

The text below is part of a letter to a newspaper, stating how the writer thinks the incidence of rape can be reduced.

In the text, there is a problem with most of the verb forms. Look carefully at the relationships between the sentences. Then decide what the correct verb form is. In some instances, there may be more than one correct alternative. Before you do the exercise, you may like to repeat Exercise 12 in Section 1.

Dear Sir/Madam,

[1. I'm write] to express my concern about the increasing number of rape attacks against women in our society and to put forward some proposals about how the incidence of rape [2. would be] reduced.

I [3. am suggesting] that the government [4. would increase] the penalties for rapists and that there [5. would be] no parole once a sentence [6. passed]. This [7. shows] the public that the state [8. may be] serious about [9. tackle] the problem of sexual assault on women. At the same time, while in prison, sex offenders, as [10. has recently recommended], [11. undergo] long-term counselling to help them [12. fighting] the problem themselves. If such counselling [13. is continuing] after the release of sex offenders, then I [14. am strongly believing] that this [15. can be] one of the most effective ways [16. reduce] the number of sexual assaults on women.

Exercise 36
Reading for writing

One way of improving your writing is to learn to absorb the organisation of a text as you read. Many of the exercises you have done up to now have, in fact, been teaching you how to do just this.

The aim of this exercise is specifically to make you read a text actively and to revise some points you have already looked at.

Read through the questions below and read the text on the opposite page. Then answer the questions and check your answer with the Key.

1. In line 1, is it possible to start the letter I write instead of I am writing?

2. Why is it not possible to replace the first sentence with the following: I read an article in your newspaper on AIDS on 15 August.?

3. Which of the following words could replace the word opinion in line 1: views/concern/belief/fears?

4. In line 3, can you write the date as follows: 15/8/96?

5. In lines 4/5, the clause As a doctor who has spent six months in research on AIDS could be left out without affecting the text in any way. Do you agree with this statement? Read the introduction, if necessary several times, with and without the phrase.

6. Do you think the writer should start the second paragraph with a phrase like: First of all, Firstly, First? Give reasons for your answer.

7. You can replace This in line 8 with It. Is this true? Give your reasons. Can you think of any other way to connect the two sentences?

8. In line 9, is the word order how would he explain correct? Give a reason for your answer.

9. In line 11, what other words can you think of to replace Moreover? Is it possible to omit Moreover here? Give a reason.

10. What other words/phrases can replace the word Therefore in line 15? Also, is the word Therefore really necessary here?

11. Is it possible to rewrite the opening sentence of the fourth paragraph as follows: The writer also suggests that resources ...? If so, which of the two do you think is better?

12. Connect the two sentences of the fourth paragraph in a different way. Which do you prefer, this new version or the writer's?

a book on **writing**

Dear Sir/Madam,

I am writing to express my opinion about an article on Acquired
Immunodeficiency Syndrome (AIDS), which appeared in your
newspaper on 15th August 1996. I fear that there is a danger of your
readers being misled by the remarks made by the writer. As a doctor
5   who has spent six months in research on AIDS, I would like to
clarify a few points for your readers.

The writer stated that AIDS is a plague sent to those who have an
immoral life. This is nonsense. I would like to ask the author how
would he explain, from his extremely narrow point of view, the
10   transmission of the Human Immuno-deficiency Virus (HIV) to
haemophilia patients. Moreover, what about the outbreak of HIV
infection in neonatal wards in some parts of the world?

A quick look at the latest information on AIDS would reveal that it is
spreading throughout the world among different nations.
15   Therefore, it is a threat to all human beings, regardless of their
lifestyle.

After his initial statement, the writer goes on to suggest that
resources should not be allocated for research programmes on AIDS.
This means a complete and utter surrender to a very threatening, but
20   controllable and preventable situation.

The article must also have been a great shock to the victims of AIDS.
We should bear in mind that people who have this disease need
sympathy, support, counselling and help, rather than isolation,
accusation and public humiliation.

25   I do hope the writer will, in future, consider the ethical and human
costs of what he writes.

Yours faithfully,

Georgina Moore.

Exercise 37
Formal and informal awareness

The first stage of deciding whether a word or phrase is formal or informal is being aware that there is a difference between the two of them. This exercise will help you to recognise formal/informal language.

Read through the sentences below and you will see that they are all informal. Try to make them formal and then compare your answer with the suggested versions in the Key.

Example:

Why don't they invest more money in the education system?

This is informal.

Formal:

I suggest that more money (should) be invested in the education system.

---

1. Thanks for your letter, which I got yesterday.

2. If I were you, I'd make a wider selection of food available.

3. Just a brief note to say how badly a member of your staff treated me.

4. You switched my flight-time without telling me!

5. Just a few words to say what I think about that article which appeared in your paper the other day. It was on sport for the young.

6. Anyway, drop me a line when you have the chance.

7. What he said was just a load of rubbish.

8. There are tons of things that we can do to solve the problem.

9. And what is worse is that you find dog dirt all over the area where children are playing.

10. The thing that really got me was the writer's ignorance of this matter.

11. I reckon that the writer has got it all wrong.

12. Firstly, you never clean the canteen floors.

13. Please reply soon.

14. Yours,

15. I'd like to get an application form from you for the clerical assistant job.

---

a book on **writing**

Exercise 38
Translation from informal to formal

You are now going to see whether you can distinguish between formal and informal language in a text. Below is a formal letter to a bank manager complaining about a cheque that was not honoured by the bank. The grammar, spelling, etc. are correct, but some of the words and phrases are not suitable for a formal letter. First of all, read through the text and make a list of the words and phrases which you think are too informal. Then try to find formal items to replace them without any help. If necessary, however, you may choose from words and phrases from the list at the bottom of the page. Some of the informal examples have been marked for you.

Hello Mr Underall,

Just a few lines to say that **9.** <u>you</u> bounced a cheque, which was presented for payment on 25/1/96, in spite of the fact that my account **17.** <u>had money in it</u> at the time of presentation. I would also like to make a complaint about the subsequent service I got from **1.** <u>one of your chaps</u>.

I would call your attention to the fact that a banker's draft for £150 was paid into my account at your branch by my elder daughter, Rebecca Merstone, on 20/1/96, five days before the said cheque was presented and refused. The following day my younger daughter, Rosie, also paid £100 in cash into my account. There were, then, enough funds in my account at the time of presentation and the cheque should have been cleared.

And I'd like to point out that I got in touch with you by phone and the chap I spoke to was really rude. Not being used to such behaviour, I was, as you can imagine, left speechless.

Please inform me what compensation you propose to offer me for my inconvenience in this matter and what you are going to do re the rudeness of the cashier.

Look forward to hearing from you when you've got the time.

Best wishes,

Ms Caroline Grinaide.

---

1. a member of your staff
2. I should be grateful if you could
3. at your earliest convenience
4. 20 January 1996
5. contacted my branch
6. I am writing to lodge a complaint about the fact
7. therefore
8. the gentleman
9. the bank
10. I should also like

11. I look forward to hearing from you
12. failed to honour
13. telephone
14. 25 January 1996
15. what action you propose to take
16. sufficient
17. was in credit
18. Yours sincerely,
19. very
20. received
21. Dear

Exercise 39
Dressing up an informal letter

Another aspect of editing a text is to improve on a draft, which requires both patience and practice.

Below is the beginning of an informal letter. The text is correct, but it could be improved. Read the text and then insert some, or all, of the words and phrases below to <u>dress up</u> the passage. You do not have to use all of the items; how far you improve the text is for you to decide. Then read the Key and see if you can find the words and phrases listed.

Please note that, in some cases, you may have to change the punctuation.

1. then
2. The first thing ..... do was ....
3. and so I went along with them.
4. very pleasant studio
5. and have been settling in gradually since then.
6. loads of
7. really
8. I must admit
9. which wasn't exactly easy.
10. a bit
11. It's quite handy for the shops and
12. in one piece
13. where
14. Now that I've got my own place
15. first
16. a few lines

Dear Pierrick,

Just to let you know I got here and to give you my new address.

I arrived in London about a month ago. I had to find a place to live. When I got here, Mohamed put me up for a couple of nights and then I found this flat in West London through an agency. There's a tube station not too far away. You should come over here for a few weeks at the end of term.

Meeting people in London is quite difficult. In the beginning, I felt homesick, but one evening I went to the Student Union. I got talking to some other students. They invited me to a party, which they were going to gate-crash. It was fantastic. I met other people, some of whom I've met several times since.

---

a book on **writing**

Exercise 40
Formal to informal translation

This exercise helps you focus on the difference between formal and informal language. Below is an informal letter to a friend. The grammar, spelling, etc. are correct, but some of the words or phrases are not suitable for a friendly letter. First, see if you recognise the language which is too formal. Then try to make the letter more informal by replacing the formal words and phrases with the informal items below. Two examples have been done for you.

1. Give my regards to	9. decided	16. getting me down
2. great	10. hope to hear from you soon	17. we can meet up
3. things	11. has not been sorted out	18. Anyway
4. Why don't you	12. walk	19. Love
5. nice	13. get through to	20. write
6. really	14. sorted out	21. Many thanks
7. got	15. getting	22. loads of
8. hear		

Dear Sarah,

I am writing to thank you for your letter, which I received a couple of days ago, and for the message on my answering machine. It was 5. *such a pleasant experience* to hear from you. I've tried innumerable times to make contact with you on the phone, but I kept obtaining your answering machine. So I resolved to put pen to paper instead.

It's really wonderful of you to have arranged the holiday to Venice so efficiently. These days I don't seem to be able to get my act together; nor do I have the time or energy to do anything. I must say that chasing all this paper around at work is depressing me.

Well, I'm sorry to be informed that your noise problem has not come to a satisfactory conclusion yet. It's truly selfish and inconsiderate of people to play music at full blast, especially when all you hear is that deep thud. I would suggest you blast them with some opera in the middle of the night.

On a happier note, a meeting between us can be arranged before we go to Venice. If it's nice, we could finish that promenade along the river and then we could have a late afternoon tea. Finally, I look forward to hearing from you soon and hope 3. *your life and environment* are a bit quieter. I would be grateful if you could convey my regards to Hugh.

Yours faithfully,

Rodney

---

a book on **writing**

Exercise 41
A writing drill

Students often learn words and phrases in isolation. Then when it comes to writing a text the words and phrases do not fit in properly, or more often than not they do not come to mind easily.

In this exercise, you are asked to think of a word to fill each blank in an informal letter. Read the text through once. Then read the letter again and think of a suitable word for each gap. Write the words on a separate sheet of paper.

Check your answer with the Key. Repeat the exercise until you are able to read and fill the blanks fluently. Please note that you are not expected to be able to fill all the blanks at the first attempt. With repetition, however, you should be able to fill most of them automatically.

Dear Doug,

___1___ ___2___ your letter, ___3___ ___4___ ___5___ yesterday. ___6___ was really nice to ___7___ ___8___ ___9___. I must say, ___10__, that I was ___11___ ___12___ surprised to learn that you were back ___13___ cigarettes again.

I know you're under pressure because of your exams, ___14___ it doesn't mean that you should give ___15___ now. ___16___ ___17___ ___18___, I can't believe cigarettes are helping you. Do you remember ___19___ I said before about all the illnesses you can ___20___ by smoking, ___21___ lung cancer, heart disease and so on? By smoking, in other ___22___, you're putting your own life ___23___ risk. ___24___, what about Caroline and the ___25___? Aren't they now at greater risk due to your selfishness? ___26___ ___27___ ___28___ you, I'd start giving up ___29___. I know it isn't easy, because I've been ___30___ it all myself.

___31___ don't ___32___ start by ___33___ up gradually? ___34___ ___35___, for instance, give up the most important cigarettes of the day, ___36___: the first one in the morning; ___37___ after meals; and ___38___ while you're drinking. ___39___ you can cut ___40___ at the rate of one a day. In this way, you won't feel the withdrawal symptoms quite so badly. I suppose there's also the possibility of giving up in one ___41___. You remember Mary, don't you? ___42___, she ___43___ in smoking after she started wheezing all the time. Now she's taken ___44___ jogging. You ___45___ ___46___ to try the same.

___47___, hope you don't mind me ranting on like this. And ___48___ you ___49___ my advice. ___50___ me a line when you've got the time. My regards to Joan and the kids. And good luck in the exams!

Best wishes,

---

a book on **writing**

Section 4

a book on **writing**

Contents

Exercise 42
Recognising spelling mistakes

Once we have written something, it is difficult to recognise spelling mistakes. There are many reasons for this: we are not careful enough when we write; we check too quickly; we recognise the overall shape of the word, but we do nor check the detail within the word.

One way of looking at spelling is to consider each word as a picture. Like a person, if you see people often enough in different clothes and in different contexts, you can recognise them easily. We all come across people whom we do not recognise outside the context we usually see them in! With words, it is not much different. You have to be able to recognise words in books, in newspapers, in your own handwriting, in advertisements, on computer screens and so on. All these different word shapes and sizes can cause problems. Compare the way you write and print a word with a printed word from a book. They will all be different.

Further, some of our word pictures may be wrong, so that we are not able to see that there is a mistake in the spelling of a word. You should not, therefore, be surprised that errors occur in your writing, especially as it develops.

As you study language, you can consciously alter the pictures you have of words. One method is by learning to recognise that something is wrong.

In each line below, there is at least one spelling mistake. Read the list carefully. Find the spelling mistakes and write the corrections on a piece of paper.

1. paragraph account apply finaly preferred definitely

2. programme execises support enviroment postpone relief

3. stubborn listning stopping vegtables aditional suddenly

4. yesteday allowed expensive temporary althought because

5. passage beleif tummy careful arrival begining guaranteed

6. intresting travelled imediately tomorrow especially

7. imagine ansering correspond advertisment punishment

8. straight restuarant discusing delightful buisnessman

9. admited disapointed tunnel threatening langauge nonsense

10. cancellation examination proffesion afected occasional

11. maintenence skilled suprise colours aproval attractive

12. fortunatly puting permenant important general

a book on **writing**

Exercise 43
Recognising the correct word picture

Spelling is also about recognising that the picture of a word that you have in your head is the same as the one you see on the written page. In this exercise, you are going to pick out the correct word picture from a series of words.

In each list below, there is ONE word which is spelt correctly. Read each list carefully and decide which word is correct.

Do not mark the book so that you can do the exercise again.

1. realy fulfil acknowlege availible esential finaly

2. benifit beautifull government independant breif studing

3. dissaray dissagree disaprove disappear embarass iritate

4. feild beleive receive plaed polution preceed practiced

5. successful wonderfull powerfull preffer greif dificulty

6. procede writen inteligent separately proceedure

7. occurred originaly posession fascilitate atempt behavour

8. diffrent refering difficult carefuly gaurantee

9. acommodation phisical arrange simlar preferrable posess

10. equiped responsable necessary ocasional appearence

11. knowledge benifited licenced acheive desparate

Exercise 44
Recognising words with a different appearance

In this exercise, you are again going to look for words which have been correctly spelt. To see if you can recognise words with a different appearance, the typeface in the lists below has been changed.

In some of the lists, all of the words are correct and in others only one or two are correct. Read each list carefully and decide which words are spelt correctly.

Do not mark the book so that you can do the exercise again.

1. irresponsible aprove dillema committee aeroplain

2. desperate separate phenomenon intention occurence

3. delinquant appointment ordinry develope correspondance

4. independence technique vehicle possibility thorough

5. computer temperature enviromental erradicate alochol

6. dictionery therfore thier permission enginering

7. teatotaller independent professor tastefull

8. conscientious management envelope February

9. frightening application detention fascilities

10. liesure perceive offensive neighborhood envelop

11. intrested unfortunatly apolegetic directory

12. occasion embarrassment casalties deforestration

13. miscelaneous aproach mischievous secretary

a book on **writing**

Exercise 45
Editing sentences with different mistakes

When you write, you have to think about many things, not just spelling. You need to be aware of the correct word to use, the correct conjunction, the correct adverb, the correct punctuation, the organisation and so on. In other words, your attention is being sent in different directions at the same time. As your ability to control your writing develops (see Sections 1 and 2), you may find that some organisational mistakes disappear. This is partly because certain mechanisms have become reflex actions; you do not have to think about them all the time! You can then direct your attention to other types of inaccuracies.

In this exercise, you have to find and correct mistakes in sentences. This time the errors are not just to do with spelling. Read each sentence carefully to find the mistake and write the correction on a piece of paper.

Do not mark the book so that you can do the exercise again.

1. All primary schools should be provided computer suites.

2. Last year the matter has been debated in parliament.

3. There are many people would agree with this statement.

4. Except from buses and trains, there are other forms of public transport that could be used.

5. Young people still seem to have enormous problems in finding work.

6. Many people are very interesting in politics.

7. In recent years, juvenile crime is a serious threat to the fabric of society.

8. The accomodation on offer is usually of poor quality and very expensive.

9. One way to reduce the increasing population is to introduce licenses to have children.

10. Thanks you for your letter, which I got yesterday.

11. Urban areas are not enough big to hold all the people who migrate to them.

12. Criticism is levelled against modern architecture many times before.

13. Fines should be imposed on those break the law.

14. More money needs to be spent for a cure for cancer.

15. It should be also made clear that being punctual is necessary.

Exercise 46
Speed editing

In this exercise, there is a mistake in most of the sentences; five sentences are, in fact, correct. As with spelling, you need to learn to recognise what is wrong and what is correct. Now, you should try to increase your speed. Read each sentence as quickly as you can to find the mistake and write the correction on a piece of paper. As you do the exercise, time yourself. If you repeat the exercise, try to do it more quickly.

1. In my opinion, news on television about violence need to be censored, as it encourages violence.

2. The affects of technology on our lives are endless.

3. After the matter will be considered fully, the law will be changed.

4. There is a little doubt as to the truth of this statement. Nobody would argue against it.

5. I cannot say that I agree to the opinion expressed in the article.

6. Though generally very confident, there are certain areas where he is quite shy.

7. This can not be done as easily as people think.

8. The matter almost was overlooked.

9. Although the proposal has been put forward before, but it should be examined again.

10. Although the cost involved, new trees must be planted.

11. If many people do not have enough money to buy food and clothes, surely something has gone wrong.

12. Many people find spiders rather frightening.

13. Nobody as yet has found an answer for this problem.

14. The patient lay in a comma for several days.

15. Within the next decade, biotechnology may transform our lives.

16. A big number of people were involved in the accident.

17. They finally managed in finding a solution to the problem.

18. Even there is plenty of scope for development.

19. It is very essential to examine the situation carefully.

20. This is no different from the other one.

a book on **writing**

Exercise 47
A teacher's revenge!

In this exercise, you need to be a little bit more active in your recognition and correction of mistakes, as you will find out when you turn to the Key. Below you have 25 sentences; altogether, they are roughly the same length as an essay of 250–260 words. Three of the sentences have no mistakes and you may also find that some have more than one. Time yourself and see if you can find the mistakes in less than five minutes. Leave the exercise for a few days and try it again.

1. Fossil remains of dinosaurs are found recently.
2. The government must tighten the law in this respect.
3. Nowadays, especially young people, everyone should practise safe sex.
4. He arised the matter at the meeting before last.
5. I wonder how can the writer explain this statement.
6. Success only can be acheived by hard work.
7. I suggest you to try working a bit harder.
8. Instead, the money should be spent on improving school buildings and to help old people.
9. If people are careful when they drive, there will be fewer accidents.
10. This is a delicate matter that has raised considerable controversy.
11. Smoking is very harmfull to our health.
12. Less people would mean less problems.
13. Should education be free for all?
14. Passing exams often depends of luck.
15. We pick knowledge throughout life.
16. The idea is certainly sound and, in my opinion, it should not be introduced.
17. He bought the stationary he needed and then rushed home to right the letter.
18. The goverment are surely responsible in this case.
19. Had they acted sooner, then the collapse of the housing market would not happen.
20. He appears to be very experienced with dealing with people.
21. We are all sensible to criticism at times.
22. I've kept a dairy since I was in primary school.
23. He had to pay a £50 fee when he was caught parking in a restricted area.
24. I often loose my way around here.
25. Recent staistics have shown that the distance between the rich and the poor is increasing.

Correcting a sentence, or a series of sentences, is very different from finding mistakes in a continuous piece of writing. In a sentence, you are working within very specific limits, i.e. between two full stops. A text like the one below, however, is larger and more complex. As the language in any one sentence is subject to many influences, your mind, therefore, needs to be touching different points at any one time, like a spider.

In the text below, on the importance of computers nowadays, there are some errors. As you read the passage think about the mistakes, which are numbered. Then use the notes on the page opposite to help you correct the passage.

Nowadays **1**. the computers are being used in so many areas of our lives, **2**. as education, leisure, work, etc, that you can hardly go **3**. nowhere or do anything **4**. without come in contact with one in some form or other. **5**. Take schools for example even at primary level, children are learning more and more through the use of computers. So much **6**., in fact, that some people even believe that one day, in the none too distant future, **7**. computer will replace the teacher in the classroom. **8**. Many, if not most, homes are now **9**. equiped with home computers, so many children spend a lot of their time **10**. surround by machines. **11**. Parents increasingly find that they are now part of a new group of illiterates – the computer illiterate. As such **12**. parents are in danger not only of being unable to help their children with their homework, but also **13**. to be left behind in the work field. **14**. A knowledge of how to use computers is a necessity for **15**. everyone in the modern world.

---

1. Which is correct: <u>the computers</u>/<u>the computer</u>/<u>computers</u>?

2. <u>education ... etc</u>. are examples of the areas of our lives? Can <u>as</u> introduce examples here?

3. Look at the pattern in the rest of the sentence carefully: <u>...do anything</u>.

4. <u>without</u> is a preposition. Is the verb which follows in the correct form?

5. There are two main verbs in this sentence. Correct the punctuation.

6. A word is missing here. It refers to the previous sentence.

7. Is the word <u>computer</u> correct here? Look also at 1 above as well.

8. You need to add a word or a phrase here to help the reader. You want to show him/her that this sentence is another example to support your argument. You need, therefore, to qualify the sentence by using a word that means <u>plus</u>.

9. Is the spelling correct here?

10. Is the form of this verb correct?

11. You need to show the relationship between this sentence and the previous one. What is the purpose of this sentence?

12. Repetition?

13. Is the verb in the right form?

14. Add a word or phrase to show the relationship between this sentence and the previous text.

15. Should this be <u>everyone</u> or <u>every one</u>?

Exercise 49
Correcting and improving a text

In the passage below, the writer has made some mistakes and there are also some changes he would like to make. Read the text carefully. Then look at the guidelines on the page opposite.

The Temple to the Winds

How well remember the very first time I saw it. To a child's eyes, the distance was great and it was merely a blob on a cliff top, far away and out of reach, but somehow the blob did not look right. I couldn't say why and it perturbed me that I couldn't work it out. I didn't think to ask what it was: so mysterious it was, that I probably thought they wouldn't know anyway.

The image has huanted me ever since.

It was to be many years later when I had left home, had been to an other continent even, that I returned back. It was on a summer's, wet, cold day with the wind lashing in from the north. We approached it from the main road, walking towards the cliff top and the sea. I was apprehensive and excited: apprehensive, because it will prove to be such a dissapoint-ment, and excited by the thought that it might not be so. And there it was, precariously on the cliff edge. **14.** *Incongruous* in the Celtic landscape, the round classical building stood proud and solid against the temper of the North Sea.

We entered; and it was more than I had imagined. Opposite the door, to which we had climbed stone steps, was a tall narrow window facing straight out into the sea. There was another opening to the east, and then I turned and looked west.

Inspite of the rain, the golden strand curved round, followed by the railway line, which passed directly beneath the Temple to the Winds. The mountains, slopping up from the beach, looked different from this viewpoint; and the hills of Donegal were lost to the rain. I moved to the window and looked into the distance that still seemed so great. For a time I waited, but I could not see the little boy, so full of dreams, who was beckoned upon the winds.

---

a book on **writing**

Use the guidelines below to help you edit the passage. Note that the guidelines are in the order that you should make the improvements to the text. As an example, number **14** has been done for you.

Try not to mark the text so that you can repeat the exercise.

1. In the first line, there is a word missing.

2. Replace this word with the word <u>just</u>.

3. <u>Annoyed</u> might be better at one point in the text.

4. These two words are the wrong way round.

5. Two letters in this word are the wrong way round.

6. These two words should be one word.

7. This word is not needed. It is in third paragraph.

8. These three words are in the wrong order.

9. Add the following phrase in the correct place: <u>through soggy ground</u>.

10. The word <u>will</u> is wrong here. What should you use?

11. This word has a <u>p</u> missing.

12. This word has an extra letter <u>s</u>.

13. Put the word <u>perched</u> into a suitable place in the text.

14. Add the word <u>Incongruous</u> to a suitable place in the text.

15. Add the phrase <u>a short flight of</u> to a suitable place in the text.

16. This word should be two words.

17. This word has one <u>p</u> too many.

18. Replace this word with the word <u>peered</u>.

Exercise 50
Learning to see mistakes in a text

In this exercise, you are going to look at correcting a text in a different way. The passage below is correct. Read the passage several times and then look at the Key.

You may want to leave a gap of several days between reading the two texts.

Through the distant haze of childhood, my school holidays with Auntie Maureen and Auntie Vi stand out clearly in my mind. Even now as an adult, my occasional visits to Farkleberry Rise never fail to cheer me up.

Auntie Maureen is a favourite of mine. She is tall and slender and wears her hair in a tight bun. Her faint moustache still amuses me; at first, it made her appear rather fierce and strict to my sister and myself.

She is, in fact, rather an exciting character. To us children, she was always such fun to be with and constantly trying to keep us entertained; whether it was playing games on the wide lawn, or launching bomb attacks on the Wendy house in the wilderness at the bottom of the orchard. Auntie Vi, on the other hand, a rather jolly and quite erudite character, always seemed to be working furiously in some far off corner of the Rise, and hanging out of windows shouting encouragement at our goings-on in the garden. Much later, we found that she was, in fact, shouting at us to shut up.

Auntie Maureen was, and still is, something of a legend in the local area, famous for her amateur dramatics, homemade jam and hedges. On one memorable occasion, she put on rather a spectacular display for us. She was up a ladder cutting the hedge at the back of the Rise. We had been acting *Breeze in the Birches*, a play Auntie Maureen had written for us, when we rushed round the corner of the house to find dear Auntie Maureen in mid-air, legs and arms akimbo like a great star.

We thought she had got bored cutting the hedge and had decided to join in our fun. We roared with laughter, as Auntie Maureen disappeared over the top of the hedge with what sounded like great squeals of delight. Never have I laughed so much in all my life!

Auntie Maureen then spent three days in bed, barely able to move.

a book on **writing**

Exercise 51
Finding irrelevant information

You are now going to look at another aspect of editing a text: finding and removing irrelevant information from a passage.

We all find it difficult to concentrate as we write. Even when we have worked out the focus of an essay, there is always the temptation to add extra, and usually irrelevant, details. This is partly because it is not easy to keep within the limits we have created for ourselves. Sometimes, it also happens because we do not know how to relate additional facts to the text we are writing. Sorting out relevant information from the almost relevant is also a problem.

Below is a passage with ten irrelevant sentences or clauses. Read the text and decide which parts are irrelevant.

Example: the first sentence in paragraph 1 is irrelevant, but why?

What are the main arguments for or against banning genetic engineering?

1. Genetics is a subject which is rather complicated for the public. As the science of genetic engineering advances, science fiction is being turned into reality and it is, in my opinion, a great improvement. Such developments, however, are totally unacceptable to a large
5. proportion of the general public.

Many people object to the use of genetic engineering in food production, and are also worried about the safety of beef products. In research centres throughout the world, experiments are being carried out to produce genetically engineered plants that can resist pests or
10. produce a higher yield or last longer. Genetic engineering will lead to a healthier diet for all of mankind and, consequently, an even better standard of living. For example, tomato products are already being sold which do not rot; so-called 'Frankenstein' tomatoes. The main concern of many people is that these changes are unsafe.
15. Safety is also a primary concern of many people in other areas of life, e.g. the side-effects of medicines. They fear that such alterations will, in turn, ultimately lead to changes in the environment and food chain, which scientists have not thought of. Scientists are responsible for many disasters: there are countless stories about waste being
20. spilled into rivers and the sea. Similarly, many people are anxious that certain altered micro-organisms, which are dangerous, might accidentally escape into the environment with catastrophic consequences. Can scientists confirm categorically that the modifications they have made to the structure of plants and animals

---

continued over page

a book on **writing** 73

25   will not affect the health of both humans and animals, since innocent creatures need protection against experiments?

Another major argument against is that the morality of using genetic engineering is questionable. Recently, the general public were very shocked and disturbed to see on TV and in many newspapers the
30.   sight of a mouse, which had been genetically engineered to have no immune system. What disturbed most people was the sight of a human ear growing under the skin of the mouse's back. Such bizarre images should not be shown on TV, as it upsets many people. The ear was developed for cosmetic reasons, e.g. to help deformed
35.   children. While everyone would agree with the aim of helping people with physical deformities, few people could not but be appalled at the immoral use of helpless animals in this way. Many animal lovers, myself included, feel that they must make a stand for the rights of animals.

40.   These are but a few examples of the main arguments against the practice of genetic engineering. There are, of course, many arguments in favour, for example a better quality of food.

Exercise 52
Another maze

When you write, you are constantly making choices about your knowledge of the grammar in a language, about the content and about the connections. You have to be very alert! In this exercise, you are going to create a text by making choices from different alternatives.

Below is a passage on the measures to reduce traffic congestion in cities in the UK. The introduction is:

As the roads in the UK, especially in urban areas, become more congested, attention is being focused on ways to deal with the problem. The best way, in my opinion, is to increase investment in public transport.

Now continue the paragraph. In 1 below, two of the alternatives are wrong and one is correct. Choose the correct answer. Move on to number 2 and do the same. In each case, think of a reason, or reasons, for your choice, and why the other two alternatives are unsuitable.

          a book on **writing**

A	B	C
1. Such investment would lead to a more efficient public transport infrastructure.	Increased investment in public transport would lead to a more efficient public transport infrastructure.	Investment leads to a more efficient system.
2. It, in turn, would lead to a greater use of public transport, provided	More people would then use public transport and there would be fewer accidents, provided	More people would then use public transport, provided
3. more buses and trains are made available and it is cheaper.	more buses and trains were made available and the fares kept low.	more buses were provided and they were cheaper.
4. This would have the beneficial effect of reducing the number of private vehicles on the roads.	It would reduce the number of vehicles on the roads.	Fewer vehicles would mean fewer accidents on the roads.
5. There will be fewer vehicles,	There would be fewer vehicles,	As there would be fewer vehicles,
6. the roads would be less congested.	and the roads would be less congested.	and less congestion.
7. The traffic would move more freely.	Motorists would, therefore, be able to move around much more easily.	The cars will, as a result, be less congested.

Section 5

a book on **writing**

Contents

a book on **writing**

Exercise 53
Punctuation names

This exercise will help you test your knowledge of the names of the different punctuation marks. Try not to mark the book, as then you will be able to repeat the exercise several times.

Name all the punctuation marks in each of the sentences below:

1. Mrs Jackson couldn't find the letter immediately, but after a few days it turned up.

2. Is it so difficult to give a straight answer?

3. The dog had been very badly treated; its back was covered in sores.

4. 'Why didn't they bring this law in sooner?' she asked.

5. That was rather a half-baked idea.

6. What a wonderful fireplace!

7. Frederick Bartlett (1913–1947) is one of the world's great undiscovered poets.

8. It's James's book.

9. He gave me a really nice present – a beautiful handmade bowl.

10. The market was full of such exotic fruit, like: guavas, mangoes, starfruit and kumquats.

11. You can use several punctuation marks in a list: commas/ semicolons/oblique strokes.

Exercise 54
Questions about punctuation

It is quite difficult to learn rules in any list; and the rules of punctuation are no exception. In this exercise you can test how much you know.

Try not to mark the book, as then you will be able to repeat the exercise several times.

1. What is wrong with the punctuation in this sentence:

    Many people will now want to know why the taxpayer's money is being wasted in this way?

2. How does the punctuation change the meaning in the sentences below?

    (a) Your nephew, who bought the painting, came in the shop again yesterday.

    (b) Your nephew who bought the painting came in the shop again yesterday.

3. Is the punctuation in both sentences below correct?

    (a) Mr James, who bought the painting, came in the shop again yesterday.

    (b) Mr James who bought the painting came in the shop again yesterday.

4. Are all the commas in the sentences below necessary? If so, what is their effect on the meaning of the sentences?

    (a) Two factory managers, Mr Jones and Mrs Blair, spoke very eloquently at the meeting.

    (b) Two factory managers, Mr Jones and Mrs Blair spoke very eloquently at the meeting.

    (c) He got up early, so he would be able to finish his essay.

    (d) Mr Cook, the chair, of the Committee, spoke, at length, about the matter, however.

    (e) The man, wearing a red jumper, is the leader of the gang.

    (f) He bought a house, a garage, a cat and a garden.

    (g) Tell me immediately, if you need me for anything.

    (h) If you need me for anything, tell me immediately.

5. What is the difference between a colon and a semicolon? Use the following sentences to work out the answer:

    (a) You need three documents, namely: your passport, your driving licence and a bank statement.

    (b) I have a piece of advice for you: listen carefully to what he tells you.

    (c) The film was so boring; people just seemed to sit around and talk.

    (d) The government can do one of three things: raise taxes; increase borrowing; or just do nothing and let things take their course.

6. Which of the two following sentences has the correct punctuation?

    (a) 'Why is it's tail so long?' the little boy asked.

    (b) It's getting rather late and we'd better get home.

7. Can you use a dash in formal writing?

8. When do you use a hyphen?

9. When you use words and phrases like moreover/similarly/however at the beginning of a sentence, or in the middle, should you use commas to separate them from the rest of the text?

10. You can use brackets to indicate parenthesis. What other punctuation marks can you use?

11. Change the meaning of this sentence by adding two commas.

    The planes made from a new kind of alloy were returned to the factory.

Exercise 55
Missing punctuation

Now it is time to use the information from the previous exercises on punctuation. In each sentence below, there is one punctuation mark missing. Read the sentences carefully and decide where the missing punctuation is. Then write your corrections on a separate piece of paper. Check your answer with the Key.

1. I wonder what I can do to help you in this matter

2. What a brilliant idea Ive just had!

3. Mr Jones telephoned early and left you the following message please ring after 4pm today.

4. It's correct, isn't it

5. He wanted to get home early because it was snowing rather heavily that evening.

6. There are many ways of going about this for example, you could arrange it through a travel agent or the airline could do it for you.

7. Should you wish to have further information, I shall be glad to supply the same

8. Could you type this up for me, please

9. Three linguists, Professor Jones Professor Harvey and Dr Boyd, turned up at the seminar.

10. Yours is much bigger but its bonnet is a bit small.

a book on **writing**

Exercise 56
Punctuation correction

Some of the sentences below have the correct punctuation, some have too much, and some do not have enough.

Read the sentences carefully and decide which sentences contain the wrong punctuation. Then write your corrections on a separate piece of paper.

Check your answer with the Key.

---

1. There was a long, dark, winding, road leading up to the house.

2. Ms Bartlett rising to address the Horticultural Society tripped and fell.

3. Moreover the medicine should have been banned immediately.

4. Its body was long and thin, and covered in tiny spikes

5. He couldn't remember when to use 'Your's faithfully,' and 'Your's sincerely,'.

6. On the surface, it sounds like a good idea, but dig a bit deeper and the problems start to appear.

7. People, like scientists and inventors often appear eccentric to the rest of us.

8. The group of children who were given lots of help by their parents progressed much more quickly.

9. 'Dont ever do that again, he shouted.

10. Fewer and fewer people came to the library. Therefore, it was decided that it should be closed.

11. In reality, its not that easy to deal with.

12. Who's fault is it?

13. We had a pleasant end of term party.

14. Michel said the teacher is a very fast reader.

Exercise 57
Capital letters

Another aspect of writing, which you normally find under punctuation, is the use of capital letters.

In this exercise, you are going to complete the rules for yourself. On the left, you have examples of the use of capital letters. Match them with the rules of use in the right-hand column.

1. John, Mohamed, Nicky	(a)	the names of rivers	
2. September, March	(b)	titles with names	
3. Freetown, New York	(c)	the names of countries	
4. German, Indian	(d)	the names of people	
5. Tuesday, Friday	(e)	many abbreviations	
6. the Thames, the Amazon	(f)	adjectives of nationality	
7. A friend told me.	(g)	days of the week	
8. Pakistan, France	(h)	nouns as part of the names of places	
9. Easter, Diwali, Ramadan	(i)	the titles of books, plays, etc.	
10. the Renaissance	(j)	the first word in a sentence.	
11. The Tempest	(k)	the names of festivals	
12. Mrs Stuart, Professor West	(l)	periods of history	
13. the City of London	(m)	months of the year	
14. NB, MP, BBC	(n)	the names of cities	
15. the Himalayas, the Alps	(o)	the names of mountains	

a book on **writing**

KEY

Key to Exercise 1

2. *Organising word:* <u>ways</u>

   General subject: [reducing] unemployment [in Europe]

Possible introduction:

Unemployment throughout Europe is a major problem. However, there are several very effective measures which can be implemented to tackle the situation.

The general subject of this essay is <u>unemployment</u>. The title, however, does not ask you to write about unemployment itself; it asks you to write about <u>ways [to reduce it]</u>.

Note the organising word in the topic sentence has been changed from <u>ways</u> to <u>measures</u> to avoid repetition. (See Exercise 5). The word <u>measures</u> gives you the focus, or topic of the essay. That is why the second sentence is called a topic sentence.

To write the general statement, the title itself will help you. If you look back to number 1, you will see that it is very similar. The phrase <u>to reduce unemployment in Europe</u> in the title implies that unemployment is high, too high or increasing. Why not use this as your general statement?

The relationship between the two sentences in the introduction is: a general statement about unemployment and a topic sentence with the organising word <u>measures</u>. There is another way to look at the relationship, which will help you to understand the mechanisms involved in writing. The first sentence contains a negative idea: <u>is a major problem</u>. This is followed by a positive statement in the second sentence:

The connecting word <u>However</u> emphasises the contrast between positive and negative, and links the two statements even closer together.

3. *Organising word:* <u>disadvantages</u>

   General subject: [using] computers in the workplace

Possible introduction:

Computers have brought enormous benefits to the workplace. However, at the same time, there are many disadvantages associated with using such technology.

The structure of this introduction is very similar to Number 2 above. Notice that this time, however, the general statement is positive and the topic sentence is negative. Again, the connecting word is <u>However</u> and the phrase <u>at the same time</u> helps to emphasise the <u>+/–</u> contrast.

4. *Organising word:* <u>Discuss</u>

   General subject: <u>Food additives</u>

Possible introduction:

The use of additives in food is a matter of some controversy. Not surprisingly, therefore, there are many arguments for and against this practice.

a book on **writing**

<u>Food additives should be banned</u> is a statement which not everybody would agree with. The word <u>Discuss</u> with this statement is asking you to look at arguments for and against banning food additives. The word <u>Discuss</u> is, therefore, your organising word.

The general subject, <u>the banning of food additives</u>, is obviously a very controversial issue; so why not put this in the general statement? In the topic sentence, you can see that the organising word <u>Discuss</u> has changed to <u>arguments for and against</u>. This is, in fact, a direct translation of the <u>+/–</u> aspect of the word <u>controversy</u>.

Notice that the word connecting the two sentences is <u>therefore</u>. If you look at Number 2 above, you will see that <u>However</u> emphasised the contrast between the general statement and the topic sentence. There, we saw that the relationship between the sentences was: (i) positive/negative (contrast); (ii) general statement and topic sentence.

In this introduction, the relationship is general statement and topic sentence, but there is no contrast. This is because the two sentences are both plus/minus and are in this sense equal. We therefore need a connecting word which shows that the phrase <u>arguments for and against</u> is a logical translation of the word <u>controversy</u>.

A diagram here should help you:

General statement | Focus statement

Controversial
+/–

Therefore

arguments for and against
+/–

5. *Organising word:* <u>benefits</u>
   General subject: [investing money in] space research
Possible introduction:

The enormous sums of money spent on research into space travel is an issue that is arousing more and more controversy. Such investment has, however, brought many benefits to the world.

We are now going to look at the relationship between the two sentences in the introduction in another way. Think of the first sentence as a unit. This unit does two things:

(i) it gives you a general statement about the subject of space research.

(ii) and it contains the idea of +/– in the word controversy.

The second sentence performs different functions:

(i) it contains a topic sentence.

(ii) it contains the organising word: <u>benefits</u>.

(iii) unlike the first sentence, it contains a + idea.

(iv) it is also a contrast sentence. The word <u>however</u> emphasises that the relationship between the two sentences is not just that of general statement and topic sentence. It shows that the second sentence contrasts with the first: <u>+/–</u> contrasts with <u>+</u>.

The two units fit together from the meaning point of view. This relationship is called coherence.

Compare the structure of this question and the introduction to numbers 2 and 4 above.

6. *Organising word(s):* cause(s)/Discuss

    General subject: destruction of the environment

Possible introduction:

> *The burning of fossil fuels has contributed enormously to the destruction of the environment. However, there are many other, no less, important causes.*

This essay asks you to examine whether the burning of fossil fuels is the main contributing factor to the destruction of the environment. It is obvious, however, that there are other factors. This allows you to use the contrast mechanism you saw in 2, 3 and 5 above.

Notice here that the contrast is different. The word <u>however</u> emphasises the contrast between the fact that burning fossil fuels is a major contributing factor and the fact that there are others. Compare this with the contrast in 2, 3 and 5 above.

7. *Organising word(s):* <u>Discuss the advantages</u>

    General subject: <u>Sex education in secondary school</u>

Possible introduction:

> *Sex education at secondary level is a much debated issue. However, such education does have many advantages.*

Notice that the organisation here is the same as in 5 above.

Notice also the meaning of the word <u>Discuss</u> here. It means describe/explain. Compare this meaning of <u>Discuss</u> with 4 and 6 above. In 4, <u>Discuss</u> means: <u>to set out the arguments for and against</u>. When you have a statement which is followed by the word <u>Discuss</u>, you should read the statement and decide whether it is controversial or not. Obviously, the essay title in number 4 asks you to discuss a controversial issue. whereas this essay title does not. The subject of sex education may be controversial, but the essay question does not ask you to focus on this aspect of the general subject.

You have already seen that you can hold sentences together by meaning, that is, by coherence. You can also link sentences together by using adverbs, pronouns and synonyms. The name for this kind of linking is cohesion. In the introduction above the basic cohesive words are <u>much debated issue</u>, <u>However</u>, <u>such education</u> and <u>advantages</u>.

Read the above introductions again and see if you can find the cohesive words.

8. *Organising words:* opinion/measures

    General subject: urban traffic problems

Possible introduction:

> *Although banning cars from city centres is a good way to solve current traffic problems, there are, in my opinion, many other measures that can and should be taken.*

The introduction shows that the writer disagrees that the solution contained in the title is the best measure to solve the problem. Banning cars is a good measure, but not necessarily the best; there are others. In this introduction, the general statement and the topic sentence are in one unit. It is possible, however, to divide them into two sentences:

(i) Banning cars from city centres is a good way to solve current traffic problems.

(ii) There are many other measures that can and should be taken.

a book on **writing**

You can see that these two units of meaning are already linked to a certain extent by coherence and there is also a cohesive link with the contrast between a good way and many other measures. The word measures here is a synonym for the word way and works like a pronoun in the sentence.

The cohesive link between the two sentences is, however, not strong enough. We need something else to bind them together. We could use the word however as in 5 above, but this time you have another way of showing contrast by using although. The cohesive words in this sentence are Although, a good way and many other measures.

Compare 6 above. From the point of view of meaning, the organisation is the same as in 6 above, except that there is only one sentence.

9. *Organising word(s):* opinion/reasons
    General subject: tobacco advertising

Possible introduction:

Banning tobacco adverts on television and in other areas of the media does provoke considerable opposition. As far as I am concerned, however, such advertising should not be allowed for many reasons.

We can have a brief look at the cohesion in this introduction:

✦ Banning tobacco adverts on television and in other areas of the media is a synonym for the whole statement in the title. Thus, it links the general statement to the essay question.

✦ As far as I am concerned links the topic sentence to the title as it shows that the sentence is your opinion.

✦ however shows the contrast between the opposition to the banning in the general statement and the opposition to allowing tobacco advertising in the topic sentence.

✦ such advertising is a substitute for tobacco adverts on television and in other areas of the media. Note also the sequence is advertising, adverts and then advertising; the change of word helps to avoid repetition. The contrast in the sequence also helps to link the sentences together.

✦ reasons links the topic sentence again with the title.

Look at the previous introductions and see if you can work out how the sentences are connected by cohesion. If you cannot at this stage, do not worry.

Key to Exercise 2

1. If you now look at the topic sentence, you can see the focus of the essay: <u>arguments against</u>. The general sentence tells you that the general subject is <u>capital punishment</u>.

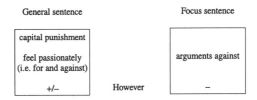

General sentence   Focus sentence

Title: *What are the arguments against capital punishment?*
              Discuss the arguments against capital punishment.

Note the use of <u>However</u> to emphasise the contrast between <u>feel passionately (+/–)</u> and <u>arguments against(–)</u>.

Now compare the structure of this introduction with that of essay titles 5 and 7 in Exercise 1.

2. The general sentence gives you the general subject in the essay title <u>[Banning] smoking in public places</u>. The word <u>controversy</u>, in the first sentence, and the words <u>arguments for and against</u>, in the second, tell you that the title asks you to discuss the pros and cons of banning smoking in public places. Note that the word <u>controversy</u> is an organising or topic word. The topic sentence then expands, or translates, the word <u>controversy</u> into <u>arguments for and against</u>. This gives you more specific words around which you can organise your essay.

Title: *Smoking in public places should be banned. Discuss.*

If you look at the cohesion between the two sentences, the organisation is as follows:

The word <u>therefore</u> links and emphasises the translation of the word <u>controversy</u>. Notice that, when you read the two sentences, you stress the word <u>therefore</u>.

Compare what you have written with title number 4 in Exercise 1.

3. The relationship between the two sentences will again help you to work out the title. The general subject of this essay is <u>Road deaths [in Europe]</u>. The title, however, does not ask you to write about this. The organising word <u>measures</u> in the topic sentence gives you a clue to the focus or topic. The organisation is:

General sentence   Topic sentence

           a book on writing

The connecting word <u>however</u> emphasises the contrast between positive and negative, and links the two statements even closer together.

Note that the general sentence states a negative idea about <u>Road deaths [in Europe]</u>. Against this negative background, the positive remedy to the situation is expressed in the topic sentence. This implies that the title asks you about <u>measures (+)</u> to improve the <u>(–)</u> situation.

If you now look back at essay titles 1 and 2 in Exercise 1, you should be able to see the same connection between the title and introduction.

Titles:

What measures could be taken to reduce the number of road deaths in Europe?
Discuss the measures to reduce the number of road deaths in Europe.

4. By now you should be aware of the fact that your introduction must link with the title both cohesively and coherently. You should also realise that, while you are writing, you must always look back to the text you have written to make sure it is well connected. If you can learn to link your introduction with your title correctly, half the battle in writing an essay is won.

In this introduction, the general subject of the essay, <u>poverty</u>, and the topic of the essay, <u>consequences</u>, are contained in one sentence. The essay is obviously not about a description of poverty itself; the topic is, the <u>consequences</u> of poverty.

With this information, you should be able to work out the title.

Title:

What are the consequences of poverty?
Discuss the consequences of poverty.

5. Again, start with the topic sentence to find the organising or focus word for the essay: <u>benefits</u>. The general subject is <u>legalising cannabis</u>. Looking back at the general sentence from the topic sentence, the word <u>however</u> tells you that there is a contrast between the two sentences. The contrast is as follows:

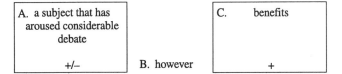

In the general sentence, phrase A describes the general subject. It also gives you a setting, or background, for the word <u>benefits</u> C.

The general subject and the topic word give you a clue to the title. It is obviously something to do with the benefits of legalising cannabis.

Title:

What are the benefits of legalising cannabis?
Discuss the benefits of legalising cannabis.

Compare this title with essay titles 5 and 7 in Exercise 1 and with 1 above.

---

6. To work out the essay question in this case is not as easy as the other titles in this exercise. Starting with the topic sentence you can see that the topic word is <u>measures</u>. You can also see from the phrase <u>Even so</u>, in the topic sentence, that there is a contrast between the topic sentence and the general sentence. The contrast is between the <u>measures</u> in the topic sentence and the <u>sound method for reducing pollution</u> mentioned in the general sentence. This implies that the title stated that recycling waste materials is the best way to reduce pollution and that you are asked to discuss it. Discuss here means: <u>describe the way mentioned in the title and, perhaps, other methods as well</u>. It is very unlikely that discuss here would mean talk about the arguments for and against.

Compare the title and explanation for essay title 8 Exercise 1. You could rewrite the introduction here by using although. Note, however, that this is not an opinion essay.

Title:

Recycling waste paper, glass and scrap metal is the best way to reduce pollution. Discuss.

7. This introduction gives a statement that is contained in the title: <u>a little knowledge is a dangerous thing</u>. The organising words (<u>cases</u> and <u>circumstances</u>) tell you that you are going to describe/discuss the areas where this statement is true or false.

Title:

A little knowledge is a dangerous thing. Discuss.

8. The general subject is <u>public and private means of transport</u>. The organising words are <u>advantages and disadvantages</u>.

Title:

Compare the advantages and disadvantages of private and public transport.
Discuss the advantages and disadvantages of private and public transport.

9. Look first to the topic sentence to find the topic/focus of the essay. You can see that there is no word that is easily recognisable as an organising word, e.g. measures, benefits, etc. However, you have the phrase <u>As far as I am concerned</u>, and <u>unacceptable</u>, which show that the essay is about expressing your opinion about a particular issue. Turning now to the general sentence, you can see that the general subject is <u>corporal punishment</u>.

Notice that the general sentence gives you general information that is neither negative nor positive, but that the topic sentence is negative. The contrast is between the fact that corporal punishment exists and the writer's opinion against.

If we now examine the title, we can see that these two elements, the general subject and the topic phrase, reflect the title.

Title:

Corporal punishment in schools should be banned. What is your opinion of this statement?
Should corporal punishment in schools be banned?

a book on **writing**

10. In this introduction, the general subject of the essay, <u>the depletion of oil resources</u>, and the topic of the essay, <u>alternative forms of energy</u>, are contained in one sentence.

Compare Title 6 in Exercise 1.

With this information, you should be able to work out the title.

Title:

Oil resources are now running out. What alternative sources of energy are available?

Key to Exercise 3

2. You can adapt **g** as follows:

    The legalisation of euthanasia is an issue which arouses enormous controversy. There are, therefore, many arguments for and against, but, in my opinion, such a practice should definitely be banned.

    You could also adapt introduction **b**.

3. You can adapt **e** as follows:

    Although many people support the legalisation of euthanasia, there are many dangers involved in such a practice.

    You could also adapt introduction **f**.

4. The answer to this is the same as number 1.

5. You can adapt **b** as follows:

    Making euthanasia legal is an issue which arouses enormous controversy. There are, therefore, many arguments for and against.

6. You can adapt **e** as follows:

    Although many people are violently opposed to the legalisation of euthanasia, there are a number of benefits to this practice.

    You could also adapt introduction **f**. Compare 3 above.

7. You can adapt **d** as follows:

    The legalisation of euthanasia has both advantages and disadvantages.

8. You can adapt **f** as follows:

    Making euthanasia legal is a controversial issue. There are, however, many strong arguments against this practice.

9. You can adapt **f** as follows:

    Making euthanasia legal is a controversial issue. There are, however, many strong arguments against this practice.

    Note that you can replace <u>against</u> with <u>for</u>. Compare 8 above.

---

a book on **writing**

Key to Exercise 4

(a) **Reasons**
more jobs/better prospects
better facilities
entertainment is accessible
greater variety of jobs
greater anonymity
more exciting
living in small towns is boring
greater variety of entertainment
greater variety of leisure facilities
faster pace of life
better health facilities
better educational facilities
better services

(b) **Disadvantages**
overcrowding
noise
pollution
health hazards
crime
cities can be very ugly
less friendly
faster pace of life
isolation
don't know your neighbours

Note

1. When some students see an essay title, they have no ideas to write about. If you are one of these students, take your essay title and make a list of any ideas which are connected with the title, like the chaotic jumble in the exercise. Do not exclude any idea. Then pick out the ideas which are connected with the focus of your essay. This is what you have already done in this exercise.

2. Above, you have the ideas for two other essays. You can combine the two together and you have the ideas for the following title:

   What are the advantages and disadvantages of living in cities?

   and in (**a**):

   What are the advantages of living in cities?

3. You can also create more ideas. For example, look at list (**a**). You can create a disadvantage by making any idea negative:

   entertainment is accessible/entertainment is inaccessible

   Of course, the same is true for the disadvantage list.

So you see the problem is not a lack of ideas, but having too many, and perhaps controlling them!

a book on **writing**

Essay Plan 1

Obesity is a problem which is on the increase in many parts of the world, especially in affluent societies. However, several effective (measures) exist to tackle the problem.

In my opinion, the most important (way) is to educate the general public.

Another (step) is to encourage parents not to buy sweets or junk food for their children.

Persuading people to change their life styles and take up some exercise is yet another possible (course of action.)

As we have seen, there are a number of (ways) to reduce obesity in rich countries.

Essay Plan 2

Whether mercy-killing is a moral act or not is an issue about which many people feel very strongly. Personally, however, I am largely against the practice of euthanasia for a number of (reasons.)

My (main) argument against is that human beings do not have the right to play God.

Another (reason I am against) the practice is because one can never be sure that the patient is, in fact, terminally ill.

In certain circumstances, however, there is some (justification) for the practice of euthanasia.

All in all, I feel that euthanasia should be banned.

Essay Plan 3

Public debate about the morality of mercy-killing has grown in intensity in recent years. There are, therefore, many arguments both for and against the issue.

The main argument against is that human beings do not have the right to play God.

Many people are fundamentally opposed to euthanasia, arguing that it is not always possible to be completely sure that a patient is, in fact, terminally ill.

In certain circumstances, however, there is strong justification for mercy-killing, provided there are strict safeguards.

As we have seen, there are many arguments both for and against.

Essay Plan 4

Exercise of every kind is becoming increasingly popular among all age groups. Few people realise, however, how much they are putting their health at risk.

The main danger is that people start exercising without taking proper advice.

Another hazard is that, if someone already has a minor injury, exercise may make it worse.

A further way that people can endanger their health is by training too hard.

As we have seen, taking exercise is fraught with danger.

Essay Plan 5

Testing everyone in the medical field for HIV would lead to all kinds of problems.

The biggest quandary would be deciding who to test.

Another problem would be the matter of cost.

In my opinion, such a programme would be impossible, because it would result in immense organisational difficulties.

a book on **writing**

Essay Plan 6

The use of animal organs for transplants in humans caused quite a stir recently. The arguments for such transplants, however, are overwhelming.

The main reason for this is that humans are more important than animals.

A further argument in favour of transplanting animal organs is .....

..... is yet another sound reason for justifying the transplantation of animal organs in humans.

To conclude, there are many arguments in favour of using animal organs for human transplants.

Essay Plan 7

Accidents in the home are increasing at an alarming rate, and yet many of them could be easily avoided with a little care.

The most obvious way is to educate the general public about the problem.

Another technique would be to attach warning labels to household goods.

Persuading manufacturers to look at ways to make certain goods safe to use is yet another possible course of action.

There may be other steps that people can take, but these are the most important.

Essay Plan 8

As far as I am concerned, there is nothing to justify war.

For me, the main argument against war is the cost in terms of human lives.

Another reason why I am against war is the senseless destruction.

Last, but not least, is the waste of resources.

In conclusion, there is no justification for war.

Essay Plan 9

Like all people, there are many things that I dislike very much; most of them are connected with living in the modern world.

At the top of my list of pet hates come mobile phones.

Another of my dislikes is noise.

Motorbikes also fill me with loathing.

Finally, people who complain all the time annoy me intensely.

Key to Exercise 6

1. a fact. Note the use of the Present Simple: <u>rises</u> and <u>sets</u>.
2. a regret (*If only .....had come!*).
3. an opinion; a subjective argument. Note the word <u>My</u>.
4. an objective argument. Note the word <u>The</u> [main ...]
5. an opinion (<u>I feel</u>); a development of the previous sentence (<u>Such/could</u>); a tentative/possible result (<u>could</u>).
6. an opinion (<u>I feel</u>); a development of the previous sentence (<u>Such/would</u>); a hypothetical, but definite result (<u>would</u>).
7. an opinion (<u>I feel</u>); a development of the previous sentence (<u>Such/will</u>); a real, definite result (<u>will</u>).
8. a possibility; an example; a development of the previous sentence (<u>These/could</u>).
9. a fact. Stating an advantage.
10. a real definite result (<u>As a result/will</u>).
11. a weak possibility (<u>might</u>).
12. a weak possibility (<u>might</u>).
13. a criticism. Note the exclamation mark at the end of the sentence.
14. a statement.
15. an example; a possibility.

Note that you may be able to give different names to some of the sentences.

Key to Exercise 7

1. a	2. b. d.	3. a. b. d.
4. a. c.	5. a. b. c.	6. a. b. c.
7. a. c. d.	8. d.	9. c. d.
10. a. b. d.		

a book on **writing**

Key to Exercise 8

1. **n**   After doing the first two exercises, you should not have any problems with Sentences 1 and 2.

   i   In relation to the contrast in number 2 below, this sentence is a concession. Join the first two sentences together with <u>although</u> and leave out the word <u>Nevertheless</u>. Sentence 1 then becomes the concession after <u>although</u>.

2. **g/h**   This is the topic sentence for the essay and contains the organising words: <u>I feel/reasons</u>.

   p   <u>Nevertheless</u> marks the sentence as a contrast to the concession in the previous sentence. The phrase <u>...totally unacceptable</u> contrasts with <u>contributed enormously</u> in sentence 1.

   l   <u>I personally feel</u> indicates this sentence is expressing an opinion.

3. **q/h**   Like essays, paragraphs also have topic/organising sentences. The organising word or topic word is <u>reason</u>. See Exercise 5.

   r   The reason is <u>the suffering that animals have to endure during tests</u>.

   b/m   The word <u>reason</u> here connects with the word <u>reasons</u> in the second sentence. This paragraph will develop the writer's main argument against vivisection.

   f   Following on from **m**, then **f** is also true.

4. **b**   This is specifically an expansion of the word <u>tests</u>.

   c   You could also think of this as a general example of the more specific example in the next sentence.

   e   The sentence could also be called an explanation.

5. **b**   This is specifically an expansion of <u>laboratory experiments</u>. Note here the development: <u>tests</u> [noun] <u>laboratory experiments</u> [noun phrase]; <u>test</u> [verb].

   d   This sentence gives a specific example of the laboratory experiments in sentence 2.

6. **l**   (See Sentence 2). There is no word or phrase specifically stating that this is the writer's opinion. However, you can see from sentence 2 that he is against animal experiments. Therefore, you can take this sentence as a statement of his opinion.

   e   This is an explanation, i.e. of <u>tests</u>, in sentence 3.

   f   This is an argument against animal experiments.

   p   Note the word <u>however</u>. The phrase <u>appalling pain and torture for the vanity of human beings</u> contrasts with <u>to make sure they are safe for humans</u>.

7. **j**   This sentence provides alternative solutions.

   k   Notice the two suggestions in this sentence: one with <u>should</u> and the other with <u>could</u>. The first one indicates the writer's opinion. The second one is a tentative suggestion, which is really like an example put forward for consideration, but it is not very strong.

   p   Note the use of <u>Instead</u>.

   l   The word <u>should</u> carries the writer's opinion. (See Exercise 12).

8.   **o**   This is the first argument for animal experiments.

     p   The phrase <u>The main counter argument</u> indicates the writer is stating a contrast with his own opinion.

     i   In relation to sentence 10, this sentence and the next one is a concession. Note the word <u>Still</u> in Sentence 10.

9.   **o**   <u>Furthermore</u> shows that the writer is stating another argument for animal experiments.

     i   See Sentence 8.

10. **p**   <u>Still</u> marks the contrast.

     l   Note the use of <u>in my opinion</u>.

     a   This final sentence of the paragraph restates the writer's opinion, which he revealed in the topic sentence, number 2. Note that there is no connecting word to indicate that it is a conclusion. It is obvious.

11.   See Sentence 3.

Note

1.   You may be able to think of other words or terms to describe the function of the above sentences.

2.   As you can see, it is possible for a sentence to have more than one function. It is hardly surprising, therefore, that we make mistakes in writing when we have to think about the grammar as well as the meaning of sentences.

Key to Exercise 9

1. j	2. e	3. l
4. f	5. k	6. h
7. b	8. c	9. i

Sentences **a**, **d** and **g** do not match any of the questions.

Key to Exercise 10

1. e	2. i	3. f
4. g	5. c	6. a
7. h	8. b	9. d

           a book on **writing**

Key to Exercise 11

In the answers below, you will see what the writer thought about the text he was writing, and then the questions he created to help him develop the text.

As you read the Thoughts and Questions below, think about the relationship between the text and the questions.

1. **Thoughts:**
    The essay title asks me what I should do 'to improve the lot of the elderly'; that must mean the teacher/examiner thinks the situation is bad.

    Question:
    What can I write generally about the elderly in the UK? What can I write to show the situation for elderly people is not good?

    Answer:
    The UK, like other countries in Europe, has an increasingly ageing population, yet it is a pity that the elderly are not properly looked after or cared for.

2. **Thoughts:**
    My previous statement is the background for my next sentence, which needs to reflect the focus of the title.
    I must also get a focus, or organising, word into my introduction as soon as possible to stop myself from wandering round in circles. This will guide me as I write, and give the reader a direction as well.

    Question:
    How many ways are there to improve the lot of elderly people?

    Answer:
    There are many ways, however, in which the lot of elderly people in this country can be improved.

3. **Thoughts:**
    I need to develop the word ways. I need to state a specific measure.

    Question:
    Can I state a specific measure to improve the situation of elderly people? What measure can I suggest?

    Answer:
    The first step that needs to be taken is to improve the living conditions of all old people.

4. **Thoughts:**
    I'd like here to say something about housing in the UK at the moment.

    Question:
    Can I give some statistical information? If so, what?

    Answer:
    According to statistics, there are over one million dwellings which have been declared unfit for habitation.

5.	**Thoughts**: I must remember that I am writing about elderly people and must not get side-tracked into talking generally about housing. I need to return to the topic at hand.	**Question**: What can I write about elderly people and housing?	**Answer**: Out of these, at least half a million are occupied by the elderly.
6.	**Thoughts**: In Sentence 3, I made a suggestion which is quite general. I need to be more specific here.	**Question**: Can I expand on Sentence 3? Can I make a more specific suggestion or proposal which is a logical development of the previous sentence? Yes, I can. What?	**Answer**: Special houses should, therefore, be built, which are cheap, and designed in such a way that they are easily accessible.
7.	**Thoughts**: I have said accessible here; the reader may not know exactly what I mean.	**Question**: What do I mean by accessible? Can I explain myself more fully?	**Answer**: By this I mean, they ought to have special provision for those who have joint problems or difficulty in walking.
8.	**Thoughts**: I'd like to make another suggestion which is a specific solution and develops Sentences 3 and 6.	**Question**: Can I make another suggestion or proposal which is a logical development of Sentences 3 and 6? If so, what?	**Answer**: Moreover, all the basic amenities should be nearby, so that the old will not have any trouble purchasing their food and other articles of daily use.
9.	**Thoughts**: I have mentioned two areas for improvement: accessibility and local amenities. Surely, heating is also important.	**Question**: What other improvement could be made to the living conditions of elderly people?	**Answer**: The provision of adequate heating is a further improvement that could be made.
10.	**Thoughts**: I need to say something more about heating as regards the elderly.	**Question**: What should be done about heating, and why?	**Answer**: These homes should be provided with proper heating facilities, as the elderly are susceptible to cold.

a book on **writing**

11.	**Thoughts:**	**Question:**	**Answer:**
	I'd like to give a conclusion which is dramatic and shows the consequence of inadequate heating.	How many old people die of cold each year?	It is estimated that hundreds of people who are old and frail die of hypothermia in their homes each winter.
12.	**Thoughts:**	**Question:**	**Answer:**
	I want to change to a new area. I also need to start a new paragraph.	What other area is important for elderly people?	Another area which requires attention is food.

Key to Exercise 12

1. <u>comes</u>. The writer wants to state his opinion (a fact) about the <u>real</u> world at the present time. He, therefore, uses the Present Simple tense.

    The Present Continuous (<u>is coming</u>) is not suitable, because it expresses a temporary action, which happens around Now.

2. <u>is</u>. The word <u>much</u>, the subject of the impersonal verb, is singular.

    For <u>would be,</u> see would in 5 below.

3. <u>think</u>. The writer wants to show that the duration of his opinion is not temporary. Therefore, he cannot use the Present Continuous – see 1 above.

4. <u>should</u>. In the first sentence, the writer described the present conditions in the world, which he thinks are unsatisfactory. The word <u>should</u>:

    ✦ puts forward a proposal or suggestion about how to improve this situation.

    ✦ modifies the verb <u>encourage</u> to express the writer's attitude, i.e. his opinion.

    ✦ is subjective.

    ✦ is hypothetical.

    You cannot use <u>would</u> to make a suggestion in this sentence. [See 5 below]. You could, however, change the sentence round to read: <u>Encouraging young people to learn more languages would be a good idea</u>. This sentence depends on a hidden condition, i.e. if the government did encourage young people to learn more languages. Note that the word <u>would</u> does not carry any attitude here; it is neutral and objective.

    You can use <u>might</u> to put forward a tentative (weak) proposal. If you look at the question itself, <u>should</u> indicates that you are being asked for proposals which you think are desirable. <u>Might</u> here is, therefore, unlikely.

5. <u>would</u>. Here the writer wants to show a result of the proposal/recommendation in the previous sentence.

Compare: If governments encouraged their people, especially young people, to learn more languages, this would bring about closer contact between different cultures and people.

The condition is in the first part of this sentence, i.e. in the if *clause. The inevitable result, which depends on the condition, is in the second part. The word* <u>would</u>:

✦ develops a new condition in some way, e.g. to express a result.

✦ shows that this development is inevitable, provided that the new condition exists.

✦ shows that your thoughts about the development are on a new level. They belong to a world that does not exist, i.e. they are hypothetical.

✦ is neutral and objective. It does not carry any attitude. (Compare <u>should</u>.)

The repetition of <u>should</u> is not necessary, as the writer has already shown his attitude in the previous sentence. He just wants to develop the proposal and show the consequences. Note that <u>should</u> is not incorrect, but it is weaker than <u>would</u> as a result. (It should, but it may not happen.) Again, the word <u>might</u> is too tentative. It is unlikely that the writer would develop and support his argument with such a weak word.

Regarding <u>brings about</u>, we are not in the real world, but in an imaginary state created by the writer with the word <u>should</u> in the previous sentence. The Present Simple in <u>brings about</u> expresses a fact, which is too definite. Look at the development in the next two sentences.

6. <u>give</u>. The clue is in the words <u>at the moment</u> as they show that the writer has now moved back into the real world. He wants to give a *real* example to support his proposal. Hence, the use of the Present Simple tense.

7. <u>could usefully be</u>. The first part of this sentence states the present reality. The second part contrasts the unsatisfactory reality with a hypothetical possibility.(See <u>but</u>.)

The words <u>are usefully</u> are obviously ridiculous. With the Present Simple there is no contrast (see <u>but</u>) between the two parts of this sentence. The impossibility of <u>are usefully</u> helps us to see the need for a contrast at a different level, i.e. the reality and unreality.

The use of <u>would usefully be</u> is not suitable. The writer is not stating a result here, but a possibility.

8. <u>could</u>. The writer is putting forward another proposal. He also wants to show that his support for this proposal/new condition is not as strong as his first one in sentence 3. He is saying that the proposal is for our consideration rather than saying he thinks it is desirable. In other words, it is a possible solution/tentative proposal. The writer also wants to avoid repeating the word <u>should</u>.

For <u>would</u> compare 4 and 5 above.

The word <u>might</u> is too tentative/weak here.

9. <u>could</u>. See the explanations for 8. The writer is only expanding his proposal, which he put forward in the previous sentence. The example is hypothetical.

a book on **writing**

10. have. The writer is talking about a state that exists already.

    are having. The state is not temporary, so the writer cannot use the Present Continuous.

    do have is too emphatic.

11. have become. The writer has moved back into the real world to describe a real situation there.

    would become. Where is the unreal condition (even a hidden one) for the would to depend on? There isn't one. Also we are now in the real world.

    could become. We are back in the real world and the writer is stating what has happened rather than what could happen, if ..... Again, where is the condition, even a hidden one?

12. would go. If there could be more informal sporting events, they .... The writer is now returning to give the result of the condition he created in the first sentence of this paragraph.

    This sentence depends on the condition created in the first sentence of the paragraph. It is the result of this condition. The sentence contrasts the hypothetical result with the unsatisfactory reality of the previous sentence. (Note however.)

Note, therefore, the sequence of tenses:

1. Fact/opinion – comes
2. Fact – is
3. Opinion – think
4. Proposal – should encourage
5. Hypothetical Result – would bring about
6. Fact/Example – give
7. Example/Possibility – could usefully be
8. Tentative Proposal – could be
9. Example/Possibility – could organise
10. Fact – have
11. Fact – have become
12. Hypothetical Result – would go

Note how the verb forms reflect the function of each sentence and also mark the relationships between the sentences. In this sense, they help to connect a text.

Key to Exercise 13

2.	A	7.	A
3.	B	8.	A
4.	A	9.	B
5.	A	10.	Conclusion for the second essay only
6.	B		

The remaining sentences put forward a particular cause of drug addiction and state your opinion. They answer the following essay question:

Drug addiction among the young in the UK stems largely from the disintegration of the family. What is your opinion?

Note

In the topic sentence, 2A, there is no noun which acts as a focus or organising word. Then in 3B, you have an organising noun: <u>method</u>. In 2A, a focus word (like approach, way, method) is, in effect, contained in the verb: [if it] <u>is approached</u>.

As you read, look for similar examples of this way of connecting. (Compare the Key to Exercise 36.6 and 36.11.)

Key to Exercise 14

13, 11, 14, 10, 4, 6, 7, 1.

a book on **writing**

Key to Exercise 15

1. **Adverbs**: besides, consequently, however, moreover, thus, though, what is more

   Conjunctions: and, though, although, if, where, when, while, but

   Note that <u>though</u> can be an adverb and a conjunction.

   See 4 below for the word <u>but</u>.

2. A **conjunction** is a word which joins two sentences together into one unit. An **adverb** connects two sentences, but the sentences still remain separate units, with a fullstop or semicolon between them.

3. The answer is (**a**); <u>but</u> is a conjunction and <u>however</u> is an adverb (see 4 below). <u>However</u> is used as follows:

   (a) The steps that have been taken are admirable. However, they may be too late to do any good.

   or

   (b) The steps that have been taken are admirable; however, they may be too late to do any good.

   Note that you may also place the word <u>however</u> after the word <u>may</u> and at the end of the sentence:

   (c) ......They may, however, be too late to do any good.

   (d) ....They may be too late to do any good, however.

4. The answer is yes and no. <u>But</u> is a conjunction, and so the text should read as follows: .... admirable, but ... Many people now use <u>but</u> in the same way as <u>however</u>. So in answer 1 above, they would say the word <u>but</u> is an adverb as well.

5. The two words are both conjunctions, but look at the following examples:

   (i) The steps that have been taken are admirable, but they may be too late to do any good.

   (ii) Although the steps that have been taken are admirable, they may be too late to do any good.

   (iii) They may be too late to do any good, but the steps that have been taken are admirable.

   (iv) Although they may be too late to do any good, the steps that have been taken are admirable.

   Note, first of all, the positions of <u>although</u> and <u>but</u> in the sentences.

   The basic difference is that <u>although</u> introduces the part of the sentence which contains the concession and <u>but</u> introduces the part with the contrast. In most cases, it is up to you which aspect of the relationship you wish to highlight. That is why all the above are possible.

   It is, however, not always possible to change the clauses around; the second sentence below does not make sense.

   Although it was –20°C, she went out without a coat.

   Although she went out without a coat, it was –20°C.

6.   You can use <u>yet</u> as a conjunction or an adverb. Note you can say <u>and yet</u>, but not <u>and but</u>. Compare 3 and 4 above.

7.   <u>On the other hand</u>. Many students think this phrase means the same as <u>In addition, etc</u>. It means by contrast.

8.   With words that express feelings, e.g. admire, approve, disapprove, dislike, enjoy, sympathise. For example:

     Much as I disapproved of the policy, it was introduced.

9.   <u>namely</u>. The others introduce examples from a list of items; <u>namely</u> introduces the complete list.

10. The words <u>Take</u> and <u>is</u> are two main verbs without any connecting word. You therefore need a full stop or a semicolon after the word example, not a comma:

     .... example. It is also a sport ......

     .... example; it is also a sport ......

Key to Exercise 16

1.   It is an adverb.

2.   You can divide the first sentence into two parts:

     (i) A man appeared ....

     (ii) ....round the corner and walked briskly along the street.

     The word <u>A</u> shows you that this is the first time this person has been mentioned. The article <u>the</u> with <u>corner</u> and <u>street</u> shows you that these places are already part of the story, picture or context.

     Another way to help you understand this is that the first sentence is divided into two parts: (i) new information; and (ii) old information. Look at the second sentence; you can see that <u>A man</u> has now become <u>The man</u> [old information]. The new information comes with the indefinite article <u>a</u>: ... <u>a shop</u>. As you write, and read, keep this old/new balance in mind. You should now be able to work out which word fills the blank: <u>the</u> (old information).

     See Exercises 29 and 30 for more information on the old/new division in cohesion.

     For the articles in connections within a text, see Exercise 26.

3.   You need to avoid the repetition of the phrase <u>alcohol advertisements</u>. If you use the plural pronoun <u>they</u> here, it could refer to <u>problems</u>, which is possible, but it is the <u>alcohol advertisements</u> that the writer wants to refer to. You could use <u>such advertisements</u> or <u>advertising alcohol</u> [... causes], or <u>alcohol advertising</u> [... causes].

4.   In (a), <u>in the end</u> means after a time and contrasts with <u>At first</u>. You could not use <u>finally</u> here.

     In (b), <u>finally</u> indicates the last step in a sequence: <u>First, ... Next ... then, ... and Finally</u>. You can replace it with <u>Last</u> or <u>Lastly</u> here.

     In (c), <u>finally</u> is part of another sequence of steps: <u>First(ly), ... Second(ly)... finally, ...</u> Note you could replace <u>finally</u> here with <u>third(ly)</u> and <u>last(ly)</u>.

5. They all indicate a result.

6. The answer is a, because the word <u>otherwise</u> is an adverb. You therefore need a semicolon or a full stop after the word <u>carefully</u> and a comma after <u>otherwise</u>.

7. <u>Although</u> is a conjunction, <u>despite</u> is a preposition and <u>in spite of</u> a prepositional phrase. Note that the verb is in the <u>-ing</u> form after <u>Despite</u> and <u>In spite of</u>.

   Although he played a major role in the peace process, his achievement went unrecognised.
   Despite playing a major role in the peace process, his achievement went unrecognised.
   In spite of playing a major role in the peace process, his achievement went unrecognised.

   You can also say:

   In spite of the fact that he played.....
   Despite the fact that he played.....

8. You need a relative pronoun after the word <u>measures</u>, that/which.

9. <u>First</u> is part of a list of points, 1., 2., 3., etc. It can be followed by <u>second(ly)</u> and also <u>then/next</u>, etc. <u>At first</u> is connected only with time. It means at the beginning of a period and contrasts with <u>in the end</u>. You can use <u>in the beginning</u> instead of <u>at first</u>.

   See 4 above.

10. <u>matter, issue, subject, question</u>. Note that each of these words can refer to the text which comes after the colon. Compare 3 above. See Exercises 23 to 28.

Key to Exercise 17

1. *Answer:* **b**

   <u>a</u> does not make sense. The desired result or purpose of tightening the censorship laws is to bring the media under stricter control.

2. *Answer:* **a**

   <u>Therefore</u> is an adverb. It can link two sentences together, but it cannot make them into one unit. (Compare in Exercises 15.1, 15.2 and 15.3.)

3. *Answer:* **a**

   You cannot use <u>Although</u> and <u>but</u> together in this way. You can, however, use <u>yet</u>, as the word <u>yet</u> is used as an adverb here. (See Exercise 15.6.)

4. *Answer:* **b**

   <u>Besides</u> is an adverb with the same meaning as <u>In addition</u>, etc. The word <u>beside</u> is a preposition meaning next to.

5. *Answer:* **a**

   <u>Even so</u> is an adverb. It cannot make two sentences into one unit. It is slightly stronger in meaning than <u>however</u>.

6. *Answer:* **a**

    The word <u>so</u> in the second part of the sentence introduces a purpose. You cannot therefore use a comma before <u>so</u>.

    Compare:

    Jane and Diva got up early, so they were able to catch the first train.

    Now you can use a comma before <u>so</u>, because the second clause is a result. Compare the verb forms in the second part of each sentence.

    Also compare **11a** below.

7. *Answer:* **b**

    <u>a</u> is obviously illogical. <u>Although</u> introduces a concession, not a reason. Note the position of the clause with the word <u>because</u> in it, at the beginning of the sentence.

8. *Answer:* **a.**

    See Exercise 15.8. <u>Even</u> is not a conjunction. If you wrote <u>Even though</u>, then the sentence would be correct.

9. *Answer:* **b**

    <u>Like</u> gives examples out of many possibilities and <u>namely</u> introduces a list of all the possibilities.

10. *Answer:* **b**

    See 9 above.

11. *Answer:* **a**

    See 2 above.

Key to Exercise 18

1.	**j**	Relationship: Concession/contrast
2.	**a**	Relationship: Cause/effect-result
3.	**k**	Relationship: Cause/effect-result
4.	**i**	Relationship: Concession/contrast
5.	**f**	Relationship: Reason/statement/
6.	**g**	Relationship: Statement-assertion/purpose
7.	**c**	Relationship: Concession/contrast
8.	**b**	Relationship: Cause/effect-result
9.	**d**	Relationship: Cause/effect
10.	**h**	Relationship: Condition/result
11.	**m**	Relationship: Statement/concession
12.	**l**	Relationship: Warning/result
13.	**e**	Relationship: Condition/result

a book on **writing**

Key to Exercise 19

1. When/Once/As soon as he had ....

2. If/If only action had ....

3. Now that/Since/When/As soon as the exams are over, ...

4. There are many things you can do to get exercise, like walking ....

5. Once/When/If/As soon as the referee sees ....

6. Although television has ....

7. There are many steps that/which ....

8. Whether the law on ....

9. Unless the leak is mended, ...

10. .... left the restaurant so that the owner could close early.

11. Maureen teaches botany and Violet teaches history.

12. Whereas/Although the number of car accidents is......................

    or

    .... , but, in other countries, ...

13. .... ; all in all the holiday was a disaster.

14. At first the violence occurred ....

Now that you know the answers, repeat the exercise and see how quickly the connectors come to mind. After you have repeated the exercise several times, you should be able to feel where you need to put the connecting devices.

Key to Exercise 20

Suggested text:

Private vehicles play a key role in our lives, as they provide independent transport, freedom and many jobs. At the same time, however, they cause pollution, traffic jams, noise and death.

Firstly, private transport, especially the car, gives us freedom to move, so we no longer need to organise our lives around bus or train timetables. In fact, many people think that their cars are such indispensable machines that they cannot live without them. For example, many people who live in rural areas need private vehicles for shopping, socialising, taking children to schools etc. Without a car, their lives would be very difficult, and they would be forced to rely on infrequent public transport, if it existed at all. That is why many families who live in the country have one or more cars; otherwise they would be cut off from the rest of the world. Hence, for many people a car is a necessity.

Notes

Sentences 1 and 2. You can also use <u>because</u> and <u>since</u>.

Sentence 3. <u>At the same time</u> emphasises the contrast. Notice the change in rhythm of the text if you leave it out.

Sentences 4 and 5. This is a different way of saying <u>therefore, accordingly, etc</u>.

Sentence 6. You could also have <u>of course</u> and <u>indeed</u>. If you put <u>Moreover</u>, or words or phrases with a similar meaning, it is correct. It just changes the relationship as regards meaning between the two sentences.

Sentence 7. There are many variations here. You could have:

Many people think that their cars are so indispensable that they cannot live without them.

Many people think that their cars are indispensable machines. As a result/Consequently/etc, they cannot live without them.

Sentence 11. See *Sentences 4/5/7* above.

Sentence 12. Note that <u>otherwise</u> is an adverb. You can have a semicolon or a full stop here.

Sentence 13. You could also use <u>Thus/Therefore</u>.

Now read the text several times with and without the connecting words. You can see that the sequence of short sentences in the original does not read very well. Try therefore to avoid writing short sentences one after another.

Before you write your own essays, read the two versions above so that you can learn to feel where the connectors in a text should be.

---

a book on **writing**

Key to Exercise 21

A.

a.	11	b.	7	c.	6
d.	8	e.	3	f.	2
g.	10	h.	12	i.	1
j.	5	k.	4	l.	9
m.	13				

B. Essay title:

Do you agree that sex education should be taught in all schools at secondary level?

When you are writing always put the title at the top of the page, as this will help guide you as you write. In an exam, if the title is very long, it may not be possible to do this. In that case, keep referring to the title to make sure you are answering the question correctly.

Note

When you have checked your answer with the Key, you can repeat the exercise as many times as you want. Try and put in the missing words and phrases automatically. The more you repeat the exercise, the easier it becomes.

Key to Exercise 22

Few people would deny the validity of the __6__ saying. __4__ the power of knowledge exerts a considerable force.

__10__ As some politicians have access to many sources of information, they possess a formidable weapon: power. __14__ they are able to control the lives of the general public. __3__, when politicians want public support for a particular cause, all they have to do is put forward the positive aspects of their proposals and hide the negative. The public, ignorant of the whole picture, __13__ lend their support to the politicians' cause. __2__, other politicians are also controlled. __5__ the general public and other politicians, through lack of knowledge, are at the mercy of the politician who possesses knowledge, and __8__ power.

__1__. When someone applies for a job, __12__, the success of the application depends, __17__, on the knowledge of the person who applies. __15__ knowledge involves skills, __16__ knowing how best to complete the application form; using the correct language; or how to write the accompanying letter. __11__, the success of the application will depend on the applicant's display of knowledge about the post applied for. __7__ success or failure will largely be dependent on his/her accumulation of knowledge, __9__ he/she can deal effectively with others and not be manipulated by them, too much.

a book on **writing**

Key to Exercise 23

1. solution
    The first sentence is a measure/proposal/recommendation/suggestion. The word solution, however, is the only one which fits the structure of the latter part of the second sentence. The phrase to the problem limits your choice of words here.

2. situation, fact, problem
    If you wanted to make a strong statement about the situation, you could use crime here. The word you use depends on how you view the situation.

3. damage
    The word situation is also perhaps possible here.

4. measure proposal recommendation suggestion idea
    The word should shows that the writer is making a suggestion/proposal/recommendation in the first sentence. The sentence also contains a measure that should be made compulsory by legislation.

    The word idea is suitable here as a reference word, but it is less specific than the word suggestion, etc., in that it does not carry the opinion contained in the word should. Note also that it does not carry the idea of action which is intended to achieve an effect, as in the word measure. It is, therefore, a more general synonym.

5. amenities
    This one is easy, because it is the only word in the plural. Can you think of another word that might fit in here? Is the word exactly what is required? Some people might use facilities, but you normally find facilities in amenities.

6. violence, entertainment
    It is interesting that the word which first comes to mind here, for some people, is entertainment.

7. measure, idea
    It is clear that the first sentence contains a measure, which is to be introduced. Notice that you cannot use suggestion/recommendation/proposal here, as nothing is being proposed. The measure has already been decided upon. Compare this sentence with number 4 above.

    Note that the word idea can be used here again. See Sentence 4 for an explanation.

8. idea, measure
    Note that suggestion/recommendation/proposal do not fit here. See 4 and 7 above.

9. entertainment

10. group

11. idea, move, ploy, solution
    Another word you could have here, which is not in the list, is manoeuvre.

a book on **writing**

Key to Exercise 24

1. practices, treatment, cruelty. **2.** issue, situation, problem. **3.** relationship, link, connection. **4.** trend, craze. **5.** option. **6.** step, action. **7.** advice. **8.** encouragement. **9.** condition, requirement. **10.** outcome. **11.** threat, disaster, catastrophe. **12.** dilemma, predicament.

You may, of course, have other words that are not listed above.

Note how the way you view the text affects the word you use. For example, in Sentence 1 the word cruelty is much more forceful than treatment. In Sentence 11, you can see the negative scale increasing from threat to catastrophe.

Key to Exercise 25

1. in fact/in effect/of course
   Notice that there is no contrast between the two sentences. Moreover, the second sentence is not a development of the first; it is a fact related to the first sentence.

2. reasons
   You cannot say causes behind. The title also asks you for reasons: Why...

3. development/change/trend/phenomenon
   The first sentence does not describe a custom. (See Exercises 23 and 24). Note how strong the connections are here: in fact – reasons – this development.

4. health
   The word condition is not specific enough. The next few sentences indicate the meaning of the word required. Note that the word health is looking forward in the text.

5. People
   You need to avoid repetition in a text by looking for alternative words. (See Exercises 23/24/28).

6. such as/for example
   Note you have the word like later in the same sentence.

7. cope with/tolerate/endure/suffer
   Again you need to avoid repetition. Note that the following alternatives are too colloquial: stand/stomach/put up with.

8. Moreover/Further, etc.
   The phrase on the other hand does not mean the same as in addition.

9. They
   This is the third time you have seen this phrase. You cannot use People again as this would be repetitive; hence, the pronoun.

10. people/the public
    You need to use a noun here, as the word you need to refer to is too far away.

11. Similarly/Furthermore, etc.
You have probably seen the word <u>and</u> used at the beginning of sentences. Note, however, that the word is not an adverb of connection; it is a conjunction.

12. for example/such as/like
The word <u>namely</u> is wrong here, as you are only giving examples. You need to avoid repeating the same word/phrase as at 6 above.

13. To avoid repetition above and in the next paragraph, you can use <u>conventional medicine</u> as a synonym for <u>orthodox medicine</u>.

14. To avoid repeating the words <u>orthodox</u> and <u>medicine</u>, you can use <u>alternative treatments</u>.

15. The word <u>Another</u> is needed here.

16. You need <u>in contrast</u> here.

17. People/The public
You need a noun here. See 10 above.

18. To avoid repetition of the word <u>fear</u>, you could use: <u>are frightened of/are worried about/dread/are afraid of/are terrified of</u>.

19. Thus/Hence
This sentence is the conclusion of the paragraph.

20. turn
The word <u>switch</u> is too colloquial. Also, look at the title.

Key to Exercise 26

1. In the first sentence, there are three nouns: <u>man/ street/cottages</u>. To decide whether to use an article or not and which one to use, you need to ask yourself several questions, namely:

   Is the noun countable or uncountable?

   Is it singular or plural?

   and

   What is the context? Is it general or definite/specific? If it is specific/definite: is the context in the text; is it created by the text; or is it in the world outside the text?

   The first sentence here is general. It sets the context for the sentences that follow. All three nouns are countable. Therefore, two of the three countable nouns, <u>man</u> and <u>street</u>, need the indefinite article (<u>a</u>) before them. The word <u>cottages</u>, which is plural, does not need an article.

   In the next sentence, you need to ask the same questions again. The word <u>street</u> is countable. The context, which is now specific, was created in the previous sentence. Therefore, you need the definite article <u>the</u>. In the third sentence, you have three nouns: <u>man/alleys/cottages</u>. Again, you need to ask yourself the same questions for each one. <u>Man</u> and <u>cottages</u> are countable; the context was created in the first sentence and is obviously specific. Hence, you need the definite article.

---

a book on **writing**

The word alleys is different. You have not seen the word in the context before, but the writer has written the definite article. The writer created a specific context with streets and cottages. He can see, in his mind, a specific picture with the cottages and the man; it is logical that the word alleys will fit into this context. Note that this is an example of the text creating a specific context for a noun.

2.   The noun advice is uncountable. The context is specific; the phrase you gave me defines the advice; it does not mean advice generally. Compare: Advice is always difficult to follow.

3.   In this sentence, we have two nouns, namely: developments/technology. The context for the first noun is general. We only know that the developments are new, but we cannot define them or identify them. The noun is also countable and plural. You do not, therefore, need an article. Technology again is general, because we cannot define which technology, and it is uncountable. You, therefore, do not need an article.

The word blind is an adjective and it is used here to refer to a definite group of people. The context here, which is specific, is outside the written text in the real world. There are other groups in the world, like the young, the old, the poor, the rich, etc. Note that the phrase is always plural. The word the connects the text with the world outside the text.

4.   There are five nouns: walk, Studland, beach, ferry and hour. All of them, except Studland, are countable. The specific context for the words walk, beach and ferry are created by the picture the writer has in his mind of Studland. Studland is in itself a specific name; it, therefore, does not need a definite article to distinguish it from other town names. Compare The Seychelles in Sentence 8. The context for hour is general; you cannot define which hour or name a particular hour.

5.   There is only one noun: year. It is countable and its context is general, as the indefinite article a tells you. The context cannot be definite, as you cannot point to a particular year in your mind; it refers to any, or every, year.

6.   Café is countable and the context is general, because the writer is setting the scene. Compare 1 above. In the second sentence, the word sun has the definite article before it. The context is in the real world outside the text. The sun always has a definite article, because unless you go outside the solar system where the sun becomes a star, the context never changes. In the solar system, there is only one sun. That is why it is always definite.

The context for the word sky is general, according to the way the writer is thinking. He could simply have said in the sky. Here, the adjective blue is descriptive; it is not important enough to focus attention on the word sky.

In the third sentence, the two nouns room (countable) and chocolate (uncountable) have definite articles. They have not been mentioned in the text before, but we know that room fits within the specific context of the physical structure of the café. Chocolate is definite, because it is the sort of drink that one drinks in cafés. Compare 1 above.

7.   The word Islands is countable and plural. The sentence is making a general statement about islands. Seychelles is countable, plural and definite, because the writer is talking about a definite grouping of islands called the Seychelles. He is not talking about all islands.

8. You have three nouns, namely: <u>bee</u>, <u>hive</u> and <u>queen</u>. All the nouns are countable. The definite context for the word <u>bee</u> is created by the word <u>hive</u>. The construction [The] <u>most important</u> also narrows the context for the word <u>bee</u> and makes it definite.

The writer of the sentence is referring to all <u>hives</u>, so he has made the context general.

The context for the word <u>queen</u> has been created by <u>The most important bee</u> and the word <u>hive</u>.

Compare:

A bee lives in a hive and the leader of the hive is the queen.

Bees live in hives and their leaders are called queens.

9. The nouns with a definite context are <u>exercise</u> and <u>blanks</u>; <u>word</u> has a general context. All three nouns are countable. Note the definite context for <u>exercise</u>, which is created by the word <u>following</u>. Also note the definite context for the word <u>blanks</u> which is created by the word <u>exercise</u>.

10. In Sentence 2 you have three nouns, namely: <u>attack</u>, <u>minutes</u> and <u>time</u>. All the nouns are countable. The definite context for the word <u>attack</u> was created in the first sentence, so you need the definite article. You cannot say from the text which <u>five minutes</u> the writer is talking about. In other words, you cannot pinpoint them exactly inside or outside the text. The context is, therefore, general.

Again the context for the word <u>time</u> is general. You do not know which <u>time</u> the writer is talking about and it is not important. As the noun is countable, you need <u>a</u>.

Key to Exercise 27

1. —	2. —	3. the
4. —	5. —	6. the
7. —	8. —	9. the
10. —	11. The	12. A
13. —/the	14. the	15. a
16. —	17. —	18. a
19. —	20. —	21. The/—
22. —/the	23. the	24. —
25. the	26. the	27. the
28. the	29. the	30. —
31. —	32. the	33. the
34. The	35. the	36. —

a book on **writing**

Key to Exercise 28

1. Paragraph 1

    a. the major events that have taken place = life (in this century)

    Paragraph 2

    b. our lives = life

    c. worlds = planets (You can replace either one)

    d. cover = travel

    Paragraph 3

    e. highly developed = sophisticated

    f. we = people

    g. everyone = people

    h. human beings = people

    i. one another = each other (You can replace either)

    j. images = messages (Replace the second phrase)

2. First of all. In Exercises 15–22, you looked at texts where the signposts and markings were obvious. Many confident writers of English are able to write without putting obvious guidelines into the text.

    In this text, you could leave out First of all. The fact that you are beginning a new paragraph, and that it is the first one after the introduction, indicates that this is the first point that you are going to describe. in many ways in the first sentence of the second paragraph could also be left in or taken out. It depends on whether you want to make the signposts in your text obvious or not.

    Secondly, you could also leave out. The fact that you are starting a new paragraph indicates that you are moving on to a second or new topic. Note the word also in this sentence has the same function as secondly.

    Thirdly, is necessary. The first idea was obvious. The second one was marked by beginning a new paragraph and the word also. Here you are beginning a new paragraph, but there is no other marker like the word also. You need, therefore, to remind yourself and the reader of how many points you have made. Without the word Thirdly, therefore, the paragraph would probably not be well connected to the previous text.

    For example, in the third paragraph, is necessary to indicate the relationship between the two sentences.

    as a consequence. (The first line in the fourth paragraph.) The word and has the same function as this phrase here. However, it is probably better to put it in, as it makes the relationship between the two parts of the sentence clearer.

3. The word ,therefore, [Many people may, therefore, fear...] is necessary at the beginning of the second sentence in the last paragraph. You need to indicate the relationship between the two sentences more clearly.

4. In the first line, the text should read the planet. You need the definite article (the) to connect the text. The writer is writing the text within the context of the solar system. If the writer uses a planet, then the context is general, which would obviously not be correct here. (See Exercises 26 and 27.)

5. Possible alternatives are:

   will have the ability to communicate by telepathy

   will have the capacity to send

   will be capable of being stored

   Note that the underlined phrases are interchangeable.

6. In the first line of paragraph 3 is bound to be and is certain to be in paragraph 4, line 1.

Key to Exercise 29

1.	g.	2.	c.	3.	d.
4.	e.	5.	a.	6.	f.
7.	b.				

Notes

1. In each sentence, you can see that the information is divided into two parts. This division is basically marked by the verb.

2. In Sentence 1, the phrase One of the most pressing problems facing our society today is not referring to any previous text. You could think of it as an introducing phrase for the new information in the latter part of the sentence (Compare Exercise 5.)

3. In Sentences 2, 5, 6 and 7, the language which refers to the previous sentence is in the first part of the sentence, before the verb. You can call this old information.

4. In Sentences 3 and 4, the old information is in the second part of the sentence.

5. Many, if not the majority of, sentences in continuous texts contain this old/new balance. As you write and read, bear this in mind and it will help you to understand writing, and reading, more easily.

After you have studied this exercise, cover the text on the right. Then try to complete the paragraph using only the text on the left.

a book on **writing**

Key to Exercise 30

1. c.	2. g.	3. e.
4. a.	5. b.	6. d.
7. f.		

Note how much trickier this exercise is compared with the previous one. It is not surprising, therefore, that so many mistakes occur in the section of the text that contains the connections between sentences.

Key to Exercise 31

Below are the contradicted facts in the text, with the line numbers indicated.

Line		Line	
1	in 1953	10	Then, in 1972, at the age of sixteen.
1	born and brought up in Hackney, north London	17	couldn't decide whether to stay in south London, where she was born,
2	the only girl in a family of four boys.	7	as her other brothers and sister were doing extremely
3	Being rather well-off,	12	as coming from a poor background she could not afford to buy many expensive clothes.
3	the family lived a totally carefree life	6	Her behaviour caused her parents no end of anguish
5	with no real interest in any school activity.	8	At school, insects, drawing and, of course, boys were her main obsessions.
6	She was very mischievous and always getting into trouble.	14	She had always been a model pupil.
11	but still very much a loner.	17	as she was known to her many friends.
18	or go to Exeter. She went to the latter,	19	as she hated the student life in London.
19	where she studied French and Italian.	21	six months in Moscow and six in Athens
22	Being decisive	22	at first, she didn't know what to do,
24	She started an acting career, which took off rather quickly.	25	After a considerable time

Key to Exercise 32

T = True and F = False.

1F. In English letters, this is not acceptable. However, you can use headed paper which has your name and address printed at the top.

2F. You can leave out all of the punctuation or you can put it in, e.g.:

Either:	27 Marylebone House,	or	27 Marylebone House
	Buffin Road,		Buffin Road
	London.		London
	SE1 7SM.		SE1 7SM

Note, however, that you cannot leave half of the punctuation in and the other half out

3F. Some people put the date on the left, above the addressee's name and address. It doesn't matter which you do. If you are worried about it, put it directly below your address, e.g.:

27 Marylebone House
Buffin Road
London
SE1 7SM
22nd August 1996

4F. It is better to write the date in full, but in some business letters you may see the date abbreviated.

5T. If you have a reference, you should put it above the addressee's address, on the left.

6T. This is true. Remember about the punctuation.

7T. Of course, this is only true if you know his/her position.

8F. If you know the addressee's name, you should always use it to begin your letter. It does not matter whether you know the person or not.

9F. It is not always necessary to begin with a heading. If you have an obvious heading, you can use it.

10F. You can also begin a formal letter by missing a line after <u>Dear ......,</u> and starting immediately below the <u>D</u> of <u>Dear</u>, e.g.:

Dear Sir/Madam,

I am writing......

You should leave a gap of one line between each subsequent paragraph and begin directly below the <u>D</u> of <u>Dear</u>.

11T. You should always do this.

Key to Exercise 33

1T. The difference is that the word <u>should</u> is more formal here.

a book on **writing**

2F. It looks bad if you repeat details from your CV. When you are sending your CV, all you need is a simple covering letter.

3T. You should avoid all contractions. They look very casual.

4F. The sentence is too colloquial. The formula for ending a formal letter is: <u>I look forward to hearing from you</u> or <u>I am looking forward to hearing from you.</u>

5F. You only use <u>Yours faithfully,</u> when you use <u>Dear Sir/Madam,</u>. You use <u>Yours sincerely,</u> when you know the name of the addressee.

6F. You should always end formal letters with the normal formulae. See 4 and 5 above.

7T. Your signature may be difficult to read. If it is, who can the reply be sent to?

8T. In a formal letter, you should try to avoid all colloquial expressions.

9F. Some people write numbers up to ten in words and larger numbers, like 41, in figures.

10T.

11F. Formal letters should be perfect.

12T.

Key to Exercise 34

1. The sender's address should have no punctuation or all the punctuation.

2. You need to write the date in full: 12th July 1996.

3. You need to write the name and the address of the addressee, e.g.:

    The Editor
    The National Guardian
    21 Farringdon Street
    London EC1

4. <u>Dear Sir/Madam,</u> is required rather than just <u>Dear Sir</u>. Note the comma after Madam.

5. You need to indent the paragraphs correctly. Or, you can start all the paragraphs below the <u>D</u> of <u>Dear</u> and leave a line between each paragraph.

6. You need to say at the beginning why you are writing: <u>I am writing to express my opinion about a recent article on fetal brain tissue transplants published in your newspaper.</u>

7. <u>I'm</u> and <u>don't</u> in the first paragraph and <u>I must say that I don't agree,</u> in the second, should be written without contractions.

8. In the second paragraph, you should use <u>however</u> instead of <u>though</u>: <u>A recent study, however, shows ......</u> The word <u>though</u> is too informal.

9. In paragraph 2, <u>in the UK</u> should read <u>in the United Kingdom</u> (<u>UK</u>).

10. In the first line of paragraph 3, <u>loads of patients</u> is too informal. You can say <u>many patients</u> instead.

11. In paragraph 3, <u>the NHS</u> should read <u>the National Health Service</u> (<u>NHS</u>). See 9 above.

12. The original text for the final paragraph is too colloquial. The following is more formal: <u>I hope that you are able to publish this letter in your newspaper</u>.

13. You need <u>Yours faithfully,</u> as the letter begins <u>Dear Sir/Madam</u>. Note that after <u>Yours faithfully,</u> you need a comma.

14. A signature is needed at the end of the letter.

15. A printed name is needed, e.g.:

    <u>Yours faithfully,</u>

    <u>George MacArthur.</u>

Key to Exercise 35

1. <u>I am writing</u>. <u>I write</u> is possible, but very formal.

2. <u>can be</u> (real possibility).
   <u>could be reduced</u> (hypothetical possibility – tentative proposal).
   <u>should be reduced</u> (proposal – with opinion).
   <u>is to be reduced</u> (fact – present simple).

3. <u>I suggest</u>.

4. <u>the government should increase/increase</u>. Note the subjunctive after the verb <u>suggest</u>. If you treat the noun <u>government</u> as singular, you do not add <u>–s</u>.

5. <u>there should be/be</u>. Note again the subjunctive (<u>be</u>) after <u>suggest</u>. You use the infinitive without <u>to</u> for all parts of the verb.

6. <u>a sentence has been/is passed</u>.

7. <u>This would show</u> (neutral/hypothetical result – objective).
   <u>This should show</u> (result with opinion – subjective).
   You could also say: <u>will show</u> (neutral/real result – objective)

8. <u>the state is</u>.

9. <u>about tackling</u>.

10. <u>has recently been/was recently recommended</u>.

11. <u>(sex offenders) should</u> (proposal – with opinion).
    <u>ought to</u> (neutral proposal – without opinion).
    <u>could undergo</u> (hypothetical possibility – tentative proposal).

12. <u>fight/to fight</u>.

13. <u>such counselling is continued/continues/were continued/were to be continued</u>.

14. <u>I strongly believe</u>.

15. <u>this would be</u> (neutral result – objective). Note that you cannot use <u>could</u> or <u>might</u> here, as they are too weak. They would contradict <u>I strongly believe</u>.

16. <u>to reduce/of reducing</u>.

a book on **writing**

1. Yes, it is. <u>I am writing</u> is more common than <u>I write</u>. The latter is very formal.

2. You need to state the reason for writing in the introduction to your letter. If you use the suggested sentence, the letter loses focus. Compare this with Exercises 1 to 2 on introductions.

3. <u>views/concern</u>. The word <u>belief</u> does not fit here. Note that you should not use the word <u>fears</u> in order to avoid repetition in line 3.

4. No. You need to write the date in full, as in the letter, or else in words: <u>the fifteenth of August nineteen ninety-six</u>.

5. If you leave out the text, there is an abrupt jump between the two sentences. Read the introduction several times with and without the text. Compare the text in Exercise 20.

6. The fact that the writer has started a new paragraph after stating <u>I would like to clarify a few points</u> shows that this is the first point. Therefore, any kind of connecting word would be unnecessary. See Exercise 28.2

7. No. If you use <u>it</u>, it is not clear what the word <u>it</u> refers to: <u>AIDS</u>, <u>plague</u>, <u>life</u> or the sentence as a whole. You therefore need <u>This</u>. You could also put a comma after the word <u>life</u> and then use <u>which</u>. The sentence, however, would be very long. You would also lose the dramatic effect of the short sentence. Note the main stress is on <u>nonsense</u> and the secondary stress on <u>This</u>. See Exercise 20.

8. No. This is an indirect question. It should read: <u>... how he would explain</u>.

9. <u>In addition</u>, <u>Further</u>, <u>Furthermore</u>. Note you cannot use <u>What is more</u>, because of the word <u>what</u> in the sentence. It is not possible to omit <u>Moreover</u> here. The word is necessary to show the relationship between this sentence and the previous text. Read the text several times with and without <u>Moreover</u> so that you can learn to feel the need for the word.

10. <u>As a consequence</u>, <u>Thus</u>, <u>Accordingly</u>, etc. See Exercise 16.5. You cannot omit <u>Therefore</u> or a similar word here for the same reason as in 9 above. Read the text with and without <u>Therefore</u> to feel the difference.

11. The answer is yes. The original is slightly more sophisticated. Both versions indicate that this is the second point for clarification. Notice the writer is trying not to use obvious markers like First/Second/Third, etc.

12. You can put a comma after <u>AIDS</u> instead of a full stop. You can then join the two sentences with <u>which</u>. Both ways are acceptable, but if you change the two sentences into one, it is rather long.

Key to Exercise 37

1. A formal version: *I am writing to thank you for your letter, which was received yesterday.*

2. You could say: *I suggest/recommend that a wider selection of food [should] be made available.* Note the contraction in I'd is unacceptable in formal writing.

3. A formal version is: *I am writing to complain about the treatment I received from a member of your staff.*

4. A formal version is: *I am writing to complain about the fact that my flight time was changed without my being informed.*

5. A formal version is: *I am writing to express my opinion about an article on sport for the young, which appeared in your newspaper recently.*

6. The formal equivalent is: *I look forward to hearing from you at your earliest convenience*; or *I am looking forward ...* Note that I look forward to is more formal. Compare I write/I am writing in Exercise 35.1.

7. Noun phrases like What he said are very common in informal/colloquial English. This could be replaced by His statement. Instead of a load of rubbish, you could just say nonsense.

8. A formal version is: *There is much that can be done to solve the problem.* Compare 9 and 12 below.

9. A formal version is: *Moreover, a worse problem is that dog faeces can be found all over the area where children are playing.*

10. You could make it formal as follows: *I was very annoyed/dismayed by the writer's ignorance of this matter.*

11. A formal version is: *I think that the writer of the article has made an enormous/serious mistake.*

12. The sentence is informal and too direct. To make it more formal and impersonal, you can change it into the passive: *Firstly, the floor of the canteen is never cleaned.*

13. See 6 above.

14. Yours faithfully,/Yours sincerely, should be used in formal letters. See Exercise 33.5.

15. A more formal version is: *I should/would be grateful if you would/could send me an application form for the post of clerical assistant.*

a book on **writing**

21. Dear Mr Underall,

6. I am writing to lodge a complaint about the fact that 9. the bank 12. failed to honour a cheque which was presented for payment on the 14. 25 January 1996, in spite of the fact that my account 17. was in credit at the time of presentation. I would also like to make a complaint about the subsequent service I 20. received from 1. a member of your staff.

I would call your attention to the fact that a banker's draft for £150, was paid into my account at your branch by my elder daughter, Rebecca Merstone, on 4. 20 January 1996, five days before the said cheque was presented and refused. The following day my younger daughter, Rosie, also paid £100 in cash into my account. There were, 7. therefore, 16. sufficient funds in my account at the time of presentation and the cheque should have been cleared.

10. I should also like to point out that I 5. contacted my branch by 13. telephone and 8. the gentleman I spoke to was 19. very rude. Not being used to such behaviour, I was, as you can imagine, left speechless.

2. I should be grateful if you could inform me what compensation you propose to offer me for my inconvenience in this matter and 15. what action you propose to take re the rudeness of the cashier.

11. I look forward to hearing from you 3. at your earliest convenience.

18. Yours sincerely,

Caroline Grinaide

Ms Caroline Grinaide.

Key to Exercise 39

The exercise is not yet finished. You can see that the text below shows you where only two of the additions have been made.

Before you look at the Key, read the version of the text in the exercise again. Then read the letter below and see if you can find the other words and phrases that have been inserted. Can you feel the difference in the text?

You may need to do this exercise several times.

Dear Pierrick,

Just a few lines to let you know I got here in one piece and to give you my new address.

I arrived in London about a month ago and have been settling in gradually since then. The first thing I had to do was find a place to live, which wasn't exactly easy. When I **15. first** got here, Mohamed put me up for a few nights and then I found this very pleasant studio flat in West London through an agency. It's quite handy for the shops and there's a tube station not too far away. Now that I've got my own place you should come over here for a few weeks at the end of term.

Meeting people in London is quite difficult. In the beginning, I must admit I felt a bit homesick, but **1. then** one evening I went to the Student Union, where I got talking to some other students. They invited me to a party, which they were going to gate-crash, and so I went along with them. It was really fantastic. I met loads of other people, some of whom I've met several times since.

Key to Exercise 40

Dear Sarah,

21. Many thanks for your letter, which I **7. got** a couple of days ago, and for the message on my answering machine. It was **5. nice** to hear from you. I've tried **22. loads of** times to **13. get through to** you on the telephone, but I kept **15. getting** your answering machine. So I **9. decided** to **20. write** instead.

It's really **2. great** of you to have **14. sorted out** the holiday to Venice so efficiently. These days I don't seem to be able to get my act together; nor do I have the time or energy to do anything. I must say that chasing all this paper around at work is **16. getting me down**.

Well, I'm sorry to **8. hear** that your noise problem **11. has not been sorted out** yet. It's **6. really** selfish and inconsiderate of people to play music at full blast, especially when all you hear is that deep thud. **4. Why don't you** blast them with some opera in the middle of the night?

On a happier note, **17. we can meet up** before we go to Venice. If it's nice, we could finish that **12. walk** along the river and then have a late afternoon tea.

18. Anyway, 10. hope to hear from you soon and hope **3. things** are a bit quieter. **1. Give my regards to** Hugh.

19. Love,

Rodney

Read the text in the exercise and the Key several times so that you learn to feel the difference between informal and formal language. Compare Exercises 37 and 38.

a book on **writing**

Key to Exercise 41

1.	Thanks 2. for	29.	right away/immediately
3.	which 4. I 5. got	30.	through
6.	It	31.	Why 32. you
7.	hear 8. from 9. you	33.	giving
10.	though	34.	You 35. could
11.	a 12. bit/little	36.	namely
13.	on	37.	those
14.	but	38.	those
15.	up/in	39.	Then
16.	What 17. 's 18 more	40.	down
	[16. And 17. another 18. thing]	41.	go
19.	what	42.	Well
20.	get	43.	packed
21.	like	44.	up
22.	words	45.	might 46. like/want
23.	at	47.	Anyway
24.	And/Also	48.	hope
25.	kids	49.	follow/take
26.	If 27. I 28. were/was	50.	Drop

You can try the same approach with many of the exercises that you have done so far. If you have not marked the text, you can try to read exercises until you are able to supply the answers automatically. Exercises 23 and 24, for example, are perfect for doing this.

Key to Exercise 42

1.	finally	7.	answering advertisement
2.	exercises environment	8.	restaurant discussing businessman
3.	listening vegetables additional	9.	admitted disappointed language
4.	yesterday although	10.	profession affected
5.	belief beginning	11.	maintenance surprise approval
6.	interesting immediately	12.	fortunately putting permanent

Key to Exercise 43

1.	fulfil	7.	occurred
2.	government	8.	difficult
3.	disappear	9.	arrange
4.	receive	10.	necessary
5.	successful	11.	knowledge
6.	separately		

Another task for you is to look up the other words in the dictionary to find the correct spelling.

Key to Exercise 44

1. irresponsible committee
2. desperate separate phenomenon intention
3. appointment
4. independence technique vehicle possibility thorough
5. computer temperature
6. permission
7. independent professor
8. conscientious management envelope February
9. frightening application detention
10. perceive offensive envelop
11. directory
12. occasion embarrassment
13. mischievous secretary

Note in **8.** envelope and **10.** envelop. Check the difference in a dictionary.

Check the spelling of the misspelt words in a dictionary.

---

a book on **writing**

Key to Exercise 45

1. ....provided with............
2. ......was debated........
3. ..... people who/that would agree....
4. Apart from..................
5. ....problems finding work.
6. ....interested in..........
7. ....has been/has become........
8. ......accommodation ....

9. ....licences...............
10. Thank you for/Thanks for........
11. ......big enough.......................
12. ....has been.............
13. ..... those who break..............
    Note: those that sounds odd here.
14. ....spent on...................
15. It should also be.....................
    Also, it should be...

Key to Exercise 46

1. ....needs ....
2. ....effects...........................
3. ....is/has been considered....
4. ....little doubt....................
5. ....agree with...................
6. This sentence is correct.
7. ......cannot...........................
8. ....was almost.....................
9. Although................, it should....
   (but is not correct here.)
10. Despite/In spite of the cost involved,....

11. This sentence is correct.
12. This sentence is correct.
13. ....answer to.....................
14. .... in a coma.....................
15. This sentence is correct.
16. A large number........................
17. ....managed to find................
18. Still there is........................
19. It is essential.......................
20. This sentence is correct.

Key to Exercise 47

In the Key below, you have to find the corrections yourself. Once you have studied the Key, repeat the exercise.

Now you can see why the exercise is called *A teacher's revenge!*

1. Fossil remains of dinosaurs were/have been found recently.
2. The government must tighten the law in this respect.
3. Nowadays everyone, especially young people, should practise safe sex.
4. He raised the matter at the meeting before last.
5. I wonder how the writer can explain this statement.
6. Success can only be achieved by hard work.
7. I suggest you try working a bit harder.
8. Instead, the money should be spent on improving school buildings and helping old people.
9. If people are careful when they drive, there will be fewer accidents.
10. This is a delicate matter that has aroused considerable controversy.

11. Smoking is very harmful to our health.

12. Fewer people would mean fewer problems.

13. Should education be free for all?

14. Passing exams often depends on luck.

15. We pick up knowledge throughout life.

16. The idea is certainly sound, but, in my opinion, it should not be introduced.

17. He bought the stationery he needed and then rushed home to write the letter.

18. The government are surely responsible in this case.

19. Had they acted sooner, then the collapse of the housing market would not have happened.

20. He appears to be very experienced in dealing with people.

21. We are all sensitive to criticism at times.

22. I've kept a diary since I was in primary school.

23. He had to pay a £50 fine when he was caught parking in a restricted area.

24. I often lose my way around here.

25. Recent statistics have shown that the gap between the rich and the poor is increasing.

Key to Exercise 48

1. The answer is <u>computers</u>. This first sentence is an introduction and is a general statement. The context for the noun <u>computers</u> is, therefore, general. If you write <u>the computers</u>, could you point to or identify the specific machines you are talking about?

   Note: you cannot have <u>the computer</u>, because the verb is plural. If you had <u>is</u> in the text, it would be correct. Note the difference between <u>computers</u> and <u>the computer</u> here. It is purely a matter of the context in which you picture the word. See Exercise 26.

2. You need to use <u>such as</u>.

3. The word <u>anywhere</u> is needed. Compare ...<u>or do anything</u>.

4. You need <u>coming</u> after the preposition <u>without</u>.

5. The text should read: <u>Take schools, for example. Even at primary level children are learning.......</u> You could replace the full stop after <u>example</u> with a semicolon (;).

6. The word <u>so</u> is missing. It refers to the fact that children are learning more and more through the use of computers.

7. The word <u>computer</u> by itself is wrong. The word <u>will</u> means you can use either <u>the computer</u> or <u>computers</u>. See 1 above. Note it would probably be better to use <u>the computer</u>, as then you would avoid repetition and thus improve the texture of the passage.

8. A word or phrase like <u>Moreover/In addition</u>, etc. is required.

9. The spelling of the word is wrong. It is <u>equipped</u>.

a book on **writing**

10. The verb form should be <u>surrounded</u> [by].

11. The sentence expresses a result of the increased use of computers in the home environment. You need a word or phrase, like: <u>As a result</u>, <u>Consequently</u>, <u>As a consequence</u>, <u>Therefore</u>, etc.

12. To avoid repetition you can use <u>They</u>.

13. The verb is still governed by the preposition <u>of</u>. You need the word <u>being</u> here.

14. The last sentence acts as a conclusion, but the sentence does not show this clearly. You need <u>Thus/Hence/Therefore</u> followed by a comma.

15. You need <u>everyone</u> here.

Key to Exercise 49

How well **1.** <u>I</u> remember the very first time I saw it. To a child's eyes, the distance was great and it was **2.** <u>just</u> a blob on a cliff top, far away and out of reach, but somehow the blob did not look right. I couldn't say why and it **3.** <u>annoyed</u> me that I couldn't work it out. I didn't think to ask what it was: so mysterious **4.** <u>was it</u>, that I probably thought they wouldn't know anyway.

The image has **5.** <u>haunted</u> me ever since.

It was to be many years later when I had left home, had been to **6.** <u>another</u> continent even, that I returned **7.** _____ It was on a **8.** cold, wet, summer's day with the wind lashing in from the north. We approached it from the main road, walking **9.** <u>through soggy ground</u> towards the cliff top and the sea. I was apprehensive and excited: apprehensive, because it **10.** <u>might</u> prove to be such a **11. and** **12.** <u>disappointment</u>, and excited by the thought that it might not be so. And there it was, **13.** <u>perched</u> precariously on the cliff edge. **14.** <u>Incongruous</u> in the Celtic landscape, the round classical building stood proud and solid against the temper of the North Sea.

We entered; and it was more than I had imagined. Opposite the door, to which we had climbed **15.** <u>a short flight of</u> stone steps, was a tall narrow window facing straight out into the sea. There was another opening to the east, and then I turned and looked west.

16. <u>In spite</u> of the rain, the golden strand curved round, followed by the railway line, which passed directly beneath the Temple to the Winds. The mountains, **17.** <u>sloping</u> up from the beach, looked different from this viewpoint; and the hills of Donegal were lost to the rain. I moved to the window and **18.** <u>peered</u> into the distance that still seemed so great. For a time I waited, but I could not see the little boy, so full of dreams, who was beckoned upon the winds.

Key to Exercise 50

The passage in the exercise is repeated below, but it now has 25 mistakes. At the end of each paragraph, the number of mistakes is indicated in brackets.

Now look for the mistakes in the text below. Try not to refer to the original text.

Try to resist the temptation to cheat!

Through the distant haze of childhood, my shool holidays with Auntie Maureen and Auntie Vi stand out clearly in my mind. Even now as an adult, my ocasional visits to Farkleberry Rise never fails to cheer me up. [3]

Auntie Maureen is a favourite of mine. She is high and slender and carries her hair in a tight bun. Her faint moustache still amuses me; first, it made her appear rather feirce and strict to my sister and myself. [4]

She is, in fact, rather an excited character. To us children, she was always such fun to be with and constantly trying to keep us entertained; it was playing games on the wide lawn or lunching bomb attacks on the Wendy house in the wilderness at the bottom of the orchard. Auntie Vi, on other hand, a rather jolly and quiet erudite character, always seemed to be working furiously in some far of corner of the Rise, and hanging windows shouting encouragement at our goings-on in garden. Much later, we found that she was, in fact, shouting at us to shut. [9]

Auntie Maureen was, and still is, some thing of a legend in the local area, famous for her amateur dramatics, homemade jam and hedges. On one memorable occasion, she put on rather a spectaclar display for us. She was up a ladder cutting the hedge at the back of the Rise. We acted *Breeze in the Birches*, a play Auntie Maureen had written for us, when we rushed round the corner of the house to find dear Auntie Maureen in mid-air, legs and arms akimbo like a great star [4]

We were thinking she had got bored to cut the hedge and had decided to join in our fun. We roared with laughter, as Auntie Maureen disappeared over the top of the hedge with what sounded like great squeals of delight. Never I have laughed so much in all my life! [3]

Auntie Maureen was then spending three days in the bed, barely able to move. [2]

---

a book on **writing**

Key to Exercise 51

1. *Genetics is a subject which is rather complicated for the public.* [Line 1]

   The general subject is about genetic engineering, not about genetics.

2. *and it is, in my opinion, a great improvement.* [Line 3]

   The essay is objective, not subjective. Therefore, the writer should not express a personal opinion.

3. *and are also worried about the safety of beef products.* [Line 7]

   The safety of beef is not connected with genetic engineering.

4. *Genetic engineering will lead to a healthier diet for all of mankind and, consequently, an even better standard of living.* [Lines 10–12]

   This certain result does not fit in here, because we are talking about genetically engineered plants. The author has just introduced the idea and then goes straight to an affirmative result, which is rather abrupt.

5. *Safety is also a primary concern of many people in other areas of life, e.g. the side-effects of medicines.* [Lines 15–16]

   This is obviously irrelevant here.

6. *Scientists are responsible for many disasters: there are countless stories about waste being spilled into rivers and the sea.* [Lines 18–20]

   Like 5 above, this is obviously not connected with the text, except for the reference to scientists.

7. *since innocent creatures need protection against experiments?* [Lines 25–26]

   The protection of animals here is not part of the argument.

8. *Such bizarre images should not be shown on TV, as it upsets many people.* [Lines 32–33]

   This sentence is not relevant, because it expresses an opinion which is not appropriate in an objective essay like this.

9. *Many animal lovers, myself included, feel that they must make a stand for the rights of animals.* [Lines 38–39]

   The paragraph is not talking about animal lovers or animal rights. The specific focus of the paragraph is about the morality of genetic engineering.

10. *There are, of course, many arguments in favour, for example a better quality of food.* [Lines 41–42]

    The arguments for are irrelevant here.

Key to Exercise 52

1. **A** is correct. The word <u>Such</u> and the <u>would</u> for result connect the sentence with the previous text.
    B is unacceptable, because it repeats text from the previous sentence.
    C is a statement of fact about an <u>investment</u> and a <u>system</u>, which are not specified. Neither noun connects with the previous text. Notice the use of the Present Simple tense here to express a fact.

2. **C** is correct. The words <u>would</u> and <u>then</u> take the development of the proposal in the introduction a step further.
    A is confusing. It is not clear whether <u>It</u> refers to <u>investment</u>, <u>infrastructure</u> or the whole idea. You cannot, therefore, use it. If you replaced <u>It</u> with <u>This</u> it would be acceptable.
    In **B**, the phrase <u>there would be fewer</u> accidents is irrelevant.

3. **B** is correct.
    A is not acceptable because the text should read <u>were made</u>; and <u>it is cheaper</u> should read <u>they were cheaper</u>.
    C only covers <u>buses</u> and the word <u>provided</u> is repeated.

4. **A** is correct.
    In **B**, it is not clear what the word <u>It</u> refers to.
    C is irrelevant.

5. **C** is correct. It is the only one which connects with the next part of the text.
    In **A**, the tense has changed and it does not connect with anything in the text that comes before or after.
    B is not accpetable for the same reasons as **A**, except for the tense.

6. **A** is correct.
    B does not connect with the previous text.
    C does not connect with the previous text.

7. **B** is correct. You need the word <u>therefore</u> to make the link firm.
    Without the word <u>therefore</u> in **A**, the connection with the previous text is very weak.
    In **C**, the tense has changed and the cars cannot be congested!

a book on **writing**

Key to Exercise 53

1.	couldn't	apostrophe
	immediately,	comma
	turned up.	full stop
2.	answer?	question mark
3.	treated;	semicolon
	in sores.	full stop
4.	'Why ...'	quotation marks/
		inverted commas
	didn't	apostrophe
	sooner?	question mark
	asked.	full stop
5.	half-baked	hyphen
	idea.	full stop
6.	fireplace!	exclamation mark

7.	(1913–1947)	brackets
	world's	apostrophe
	poets.	full stop
8.	It's	apostrophe
	James's	apostrophe
	book.	full stop
9.	– a beautiful	dash
	bowl.	full stop
10.	fruit,	comma
	like:	colon
	guavas, mangoes,	commas
	kumquats.	full stop
11.	list:	colon
	commas/	oblique stroke
	oblique strokes.	full stop

Key to Exercise 54

1. The sentence is not a question. The word why introduces an indirect question; therefore, a question mark is not needed.

2. In **a**, the text between the commas is additional information. The words could, in fact, be left out; they are not identifying which nephew. In **b**, the writer shows that there are other nephews and that he is only talking about the one who bought the painting. The words who bought the painting are essential to the meaning in **b**.

3. Sentence **b** is impossible, because the name Mr James already defines the person.

4. (a) The punctuation shows that two people spoke, Mr Jones and Mrs Blair.

   (b) Four people spoke, namely: two managers, Mr Jones, and Mrs Blair. The first two people are not named.

   (c) The comma after early is unnecessary as the second clause is a purpose. If the sentence read so he was able to finish his essay, the second clause would be a result. A comma would then be necessary.

   (d) You do not need a comma after chair, spoke and length.

   (e) The commas in the sentence should be removed as the phrase wearing a red jumper identifies the man as the leader. Compare 2 above.

   (f) All the commas are necessary.

   (g) You do not need a comma here. Read the sentence to yourself and compare it with **h** below.

   (h) When you turn the sentence in **g** round as here, you need a comma.

a book on **writing**

5. **A semicolon**

A semicolon marks a connection between two independent clauses which are related to each other, e.g. **c**. If you had a full stop instead of a semicolon in **c**, the sentences would be too staccato (i.e. abrupt, clipped). Hence, another reason for using a semicolon. You can use a semicolon to mark clauses in a list, e.g. **d**.

A colon

A colon marks an explanation of a word or clause which comes before it, e.g. **b**. You can use a colon to mark the beginning of a list, e.g. **a/d**.

6. It's means It is/It has. So **a** is incorrect.

7. A dash is usually quite informal, but people do use it in formal writing.

8. You use a hyphen to mark certain words which are made from: (i) two or more words, e.g. half-dead self-made (ii) a prefix and a word, e.g. semi-nomadic, co-ordinate.

9. Yes. You normally separate connecting words like these from the rest of the sentence with commas.

10. You can use commas (,....,) and dashes (–.....–).

11. You can write: The planes, made from a new kind of alloy, were returned to the factory. This means that all the planes were returned. Without commas, it means that only those planes made from alloy were returned. The others were not.

Key to Exercise 55

1. The full stop at the end of the sentence is missing. Notice the sentence contains an indirect question. Therefore, you do not need a question mark.

2. The apostrophe is missing in I've.

3. You need a colon after message. The latter part of the sentence is an explanation of the word message. In informal writing, you could have a dash.

4. You need a question mark at the end of the sentence.

5. A comma is needed after early.

6. You need a full stop or a semicolon after the word this. After a full stop, the word for would have a capital letter.

7. You need a full stop at the end of the sentence. Note that this is not a question. The inversion at the beginning of the sentence is the same as If you wish ... .

8. This is a question not a statement, so you need a question mark at the end.

9. You need a comma after Jones.

10. A comma is needed before but.

a book on **writing**

Key to Exercise 56

1. You do not need a comma after <u>winding</u>.

2. The phrase <u>, rising to address the Horticultural Society,</u> is non-defining. It is additional information and does not distinguish <u>Ms Bartlett</u> from anyone else. Therefore, you should put the phrase inside commas.

3. You should add a comma after <u>Moreover</u>.

4. A full stop is needed at the end of the sentence. The writer considers the information in the latter part of the sentence as additional, so you can have a comma before the word <u>and</u>. You can also leave the comma out.

5. You can't use an apostrophe with <u>Yours</u>.

6. The punctuation is correct.

7. There should not be a comma after <u>people</u>. The phrase <u>like scientists and inventors</u> is defining. Read the sentence to yourself without the phrase; it doesn't make sense.

8. You can put commas around the clause <u>who were given lots of help by their parents</u> or you can leave them out. It depends on whether you want to talk about a restricted group of children (defining) or to give additional information (non-defining).

9. An apostrophe is needed in <u>Don't</u>; you also need an exclamation mark instead of a comma. After the comma, you should close the quotation <u>: .... again!' he shouted</u>.

10. The punctuation is correct.

11. The apostrophe is missing in <u>it's: it is</u>.

12. Not only is the punctuation wrong, the word is wrong. The word should be <u>Whose</u> and there is no apostrophe.

13. Hyphens are needed in <u>end-of-term</u>.

14. The punctuation is correct, but notice the change in meaning in the following: <u>'Michel,' said the teacher, 'is a very fast reader.'</u>

Key to Exercise 57

1. d	2. m	3. n
4. f	5. g	6. a
7. j	8. c	9. k
10. l	11. i	12. b
13. h	14. e	15. o

a book on **writing**

139